☆ ☆ ☆

The Real Witches' Kitchen

☆ ☆ ☆

†

☆ ☆ ☆

Other titles by the same author

The Real Witches' Handbook

✩ ✦ ✩

The Real Witches' Kitchen

✩ ✦ ✩

SPELLS, RECIPES, OILS, LOTIONS AND
POTIONS FROM THE WITCHES' HEARTH

Kate West

Element
An Imprint of HarperCollins*Publishers*
77–85 Fulham Palace Road
Hammersmith, London W6 8JB

The website address is: www.thorsonselement.co.uk

and *Element* are trademarks of
HarperCollins*Publishers* Limited

First published by Thorsons, an Imprint of HarperCollinsPublishers 2002
This edition published by Element 2002

11

A catalogue record for this book
is available from the British Library

ISBN-13   978-0-00-711786-4
ISBN-10   0-00-711786-8

Illustrations by Chris Down

Printed in Great Britain by
Martins the Printers, Berwick upon Tweed

☆ ☆ ☆

Contents

Acknowledgements

Everything in life is made easier with the love and assistance of friends and family, and whenever you get help it's a good idea to say thank you, so here goes!

Grateful thanks go to Debbie, Julie B, Keith, Lizzie, Sybil, Steve and all the others who either proofread the text or tried out the recipes; Julie, Thelma and those others who contributed ideas, suggestions and references; and especially to Ken for the world's best Bara Brith recipe – long may it continue to grace our Sabbats.

Special thanks go to the members of the Hearth of Hecate, the Covenant of Aradia and the Children of Artemis for their unfailing support, especially through the dark times when the words wouldn't come, and most especially to Julie B, Debbie, Natalie and Thys for distracting or even removing the child!

Loving thanks to my High Priest, partner and husband Steve, as well as to Tali and, more recently, Thys for their forbearance.

And finally, thank you to everyone at Thorsons for their patience, encouragement and support.

Introduction

Merry Meet!

And welcome to *The Real Witches' Kitchen*. The image of a Witch as a ragged-haired woman, dressed all in black, throwing strange ingredients into a bubbling cauldron in the dead of night is somewhat outdated! These days she, or he, is far more likely to be someone you know, dressed in normal clothes, working in their own kitchen. Witchcraft (or the Craft) is a very practical path, so who is going to forego the convenience of a modern cooker, the cleanliness of a decent work surface or the comfort of their own home for the environment that our predecessors were obliged to make do with? A herbal remedy, candle or incense is not going to be any less effective because you created it in the kitchen at lunchtime rather than in the woods at night. Witches of old may have needed to work furtively without modern power and water supplies, but that was because of the times they lived in, not because it makes for better Magic.

This book, however, is not just about Witchcraft or just for Witches. More and more people today are looking for natural remedies to enhance their physical, emotional and spiritual well-being. They are seeking ways of enhancing their health, bodies and lives in ways which do not involve chemicals but rather make use of the herbs and plants which are all around us.

The Real Witches' Kitchen is a book for everyone who wants to start making use of nature's healing store. Here we look at the ways that common herbs and spices, and even some unlikely-sounding plants, can not only enliven our diet but also be used to heal the body, soothe the mind and enliven the spirit. Whilst this is not a cookery book, there are recipes and menus which can be used to celebrate the seasons, help our bodies to combat common ailments and even enhance romantic moments. There are teas, brews and even alcoholic beverages for celebration and for healing. There are soaps, oils, lotions and potions to smooth the way in daily life, as well as dietary advice and guidance, grooming and cosmetic tips to help you make the most of what nature has given you and candles and incenses to create a mood or focus you in the direction you need. There are even ideas for gifts for those who are dear to you.

Those who practise the Craft will find new ideas for celebrating the Wheel of the Year and ways of honouring the Goddess and the God. There are ways of feeding the elements within and working towards balance. Here you will find soaps and bathing preparations to ready yourself for the Circle, anointing oils for yourself and for Magical work, candles to carry your intent and incenses to please the Gods. There are sachets and charms, wards of protection and ways of enhancing your fortunes.

Those of you who are reading this without any previous knowledge of the Craft or who find the term 'Witchcraft' disturbing will find a very basic introduction to this largely misunderstood belief system in Chapter One, 'Witchcraft, and Empowering your Herbal Work'. This chapter will also provide guidance on using Magic to enhance the effectiveness of your work if you are new to the Craft. If you would like a more in-depth understanding, then I recommend that you also read *The Real Witches' Handbook*, together with some of the other books mentioned in the Further Information section at the end of this book.

Whatever your beliefs or spiritual path, here you will find ways of working with nature and walking more lightly on our world to make a positive difference to your physical, emotional and spiritual life.

Blessed Be

Kate

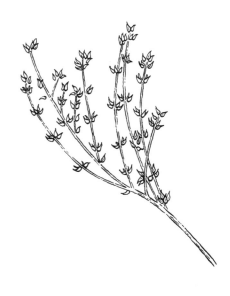

Witchcraft, and Empowering your Herbal Work

'Let the Magic come to life...'

   You do not have to be a practising Witch to make use of the recipes and skills which are covered here, but it will help if you have an understanding of the principles of the Craft. For some this will mean putting aside the misconceptions created by the media (especially the popular press) and the adverse comments made by those who have no understanding and no desire to understand our heritage.

Witchcraft is one of a number of belief systems whose roots pre-date Christianity and which come under the 'umbrella' heading of Pagan. Indeed, Witchcraft has roots which go back to Palaeolithic times, as illustrated by the cave paintings of our ancient ancestors. Having said that, the Craft is a living religion and has as much relevance to us today as it had to its practitioners in the past. We still seek healing of our bodies and minds, strength to deal with our daily lives, understanding and compassion to help us relate to those around us and to develop our own selves.

So what do Witches believe in and how do they express these beliefs? First, you have to understand that, unlike the more 'orthodox' religions, the Craft has no paid or formal priesthood; we are each our own Priest or Priestess and therefore make our own decisions as to the expression of our beliefs. As a result there is no 'one true way' to being a Witch. This gives rise to a great diversity in our daily practices and indeed enables the Craft to grow and adapt to the real world in a way that other paths find difficult because of their interpreted doctrine. Having said that, there are many beliefs and practices that most Witches hold in common:

★ We believe that the Divine is both male and female.

We believe this is equal and in balance, and that we should seek that balance in ourselves and in our lives. Put simply, this means that we believe in the Goddess and the God, and they may be referred to by many names according to the needs of the individual or indeed their personal preference. It helps to think of the Divine as being like a mirror ball, with each facet having a different identity, although all are part of the Divine. As a result you may find that the Goddess is referred to as Isis, Astarte or Hecate, for example, and the God referred to as Osiris, Herne or Pan, and so on. Some Witches will simply refer to the Lord and Lady or the Goddess and the God, and these are the terms that I will use in this book. Others will call them the Old Ones or the Old Gods, or even just the Gods.

The Goddess is seen as having three aspects: Maiden, Mother and Crone (or Wise One). These aspects are reflected in the cycle of the Moon, and in our daily lives, for everything has its beginning, middle and closing phases.

The God also has different aspects, but these are more clearly defined through the festivals of the seasons and the Wheel of the Year.

★ We are each our own Priest or Priestess.

As mentioned above we have no formal priesthood in the Craft although those Witches working in a group or Coven setting will have a High Priestess and High Priest who are the leaders of that group. This does not make them better Witches, it simply denotes their standing and authority within that group. Having no formal priesthood means we do not rely on others to interpret or intercede with our Gods for us, we are each entitled to make our own connection with the Divine in our own way. This might be through ritual, meditation and/or Magic and most Witches will use a combination of different techniques at different times.

★ We have no 'book of instruction'.

We do not have a book in the way that Christians have the Bible or Muslims the Koran. There are a great number of books on the Craft, however, and it is up to those who wish to read some of these to make personal decisions as to their relevance. Each individual can choose the complexity of their rituals, and the form that their path will take. For some this may mean working in a group or Coven, others may prefer a Solitary path. Some will seek to work formalized Magic whilst others prefer the Hedgewitch approach, working closely with nature and using herbs to achieve their Magic.

★ Everyone is entitled to their own, informed, choice of spiritual path, so long as they harm no one.

Witchcraft is a non-proselytizing belief system – we do not feel the need for everyone to believe as we do in order to feel secure in our faith. There is plenty of room in this world for everyone to find their own way of relating to the Divine. In fact all religions have as much, if not more, in common than in difference. Hence there is no reason why we should not encourage and celebrate a diversity of beliefs. We encourage our young to examine many paths and to make their own decisions, based on their own needs. We do not seek to convert others to our beliefs, nor do we wish to be indoctrinated in turn.

★ We believe that we should respect nature.

This means not taking more than we need and, indeed, trying to make recompense for that which we have taken. It involves trying to live not only in the modern world but also in balance with the planet. Witches tend to shop second-hand, make at least some of the things they use and to recycle where they can. This does not mean that we are all 'green warriors' campaigning against the building of roads or houses. It does mean that we try to tread lightly on the world.

★ Witches utilize the elements in their workings.

It is not just that we respect nature, we also see ourselves reflected by the elements of Air, Fire, Water, Earth and Spirit. Whilst these elements are all around us in nature they are also within us: Air is our thoughts, Fire our passions and enthusiasm, Water our emotions, Earth our bodies and Spirit our inner selves. These are the energies we harness in working Magic and in order for this to be effective we must be able to achieve balance between them. These elements also have their reflections in daily life. For every project to work it must have its phases of thought, enthusiasm, emotional involvement and formation, and must also be imbued with its own spirit.

★ We believe in and practise Magic.

Magic has been defined as the ability to create change by force of will and in some respects is not dissimilar to a belief in the power of prayer. However, in Magic it is our personal intervention which creates the change around us. Magic is not like cookery, just a matter of following a recipe and getting a result. True Magic requires a deep understanding of ourselves and the energies that are around us, and the ability to control and focus our own energies. One of the greatest keys to this is the ability to visualize. It also requires a study and understanding of the elements of Earth, Air, Fire and Water, not just in the world, but also within ourselves.

The Magic we practise is not that of stage conjuring or of the special effects that you see so often in modern films. It is practised to heal, protect and enhance our lives. It is worked for ourselves, our near and dear, and for those who come to us with requests for help. Magic should always be practised with the Wiccan Rede ('An' it harm none, do what thou will') in mind and also with regard to the Law of Threefold Return which states that whatever you do, good or ill, will be returned to you three times over. This latter is not confined to Magical working, but should be borne in mind at all times. If you are careful to harm no one and not to interfere with anyone's freedom of will, then you have the basic guidelines for good Magical practice.

★ Witches celebrate the Wheel of the Year.

The Witches' calendar contains eight key festivals, called Sabbats. At these we mark the changes of the seasons and the stories of the Goddess and the God. Whenever possible Witches will gather together to celebrate these festivals by dancing, singing and honouring the Goddess and the God by re-enacting their stories, but Solitary Witches also mark the Sabbats. At the end of these rituals we celebrate by feasting with food and wine. Many of the Sabbats have a familiar feel to non-Witches as they have been taken over by newer belief systems and incorporated into their calendars. Briefly the Sabbats are:

Samhain, 31 October. The most important festival, marking the beginning and end of the year, the beginning of the resting season of the land and a time of remembrance of those who have gone before. A feast of the Goddess as Crone and Wise One.

Yule, 21 December. The Winter Solstice when the decreasing days give way to increasing light and life and we celebrate the rebirth of the Sun.

Imbolg, 2 February. The time when the first signs of life are seen returning to the land and the Goddess changes her robes of Crone for those of Maiden.

Oestara, 21 March. The Spring Equinox, when day and night are equal. The festival of the Goddess Eostar, who is derived from the Goddess Astarte, and whose symbols are the egg and the hare.

Beltane, 1 May. The second most important festival of the year, when the Goddess changes her robes of Maiden for those of Mother and we celebrate the marriage of the Goddess and the God.

Litha, 21 June. The Summer Solstice. Here the Sun is at the peak of its power; from this time onwards the days gradually grow shorter again.

Lammas, 1 August. The festival of the first of the harvest. The feast of Lugh and of the Sacrificial King, who is these days most often represented by a gingerbread man.

Madron, 21 September. The Autumn Equinox, once more a time of balance when day and night are equal. The feast of the height of the harvest.

On the return to Samhain the year has turned full circle, hence the term 'Wheel of the Year'. In this book you will find recipes for wines, breads, cakes, biscuits (cookies) and other feasting food to celebrate each of these festivals. You do not have to reserve these celebratory aspects of the Craft to share with others on the Path, you can share them with friends and family as a seasonal celebration, so long as you remember not to use this as an opportunity to preach in any way!

People living in the Southern Hemisphere will find their seasons are reversed and may prefer to celebrate the Sabbats as appropriate to the season rather than the calendar date.

★ We take personal responsibility for our lives.

The main 'rule' in the Craft is called the Wiccan Rede: 'An it harm none, do what thou will.' This in itself includes not only respect for others and the world around us, but also respect for ourselves. We believe that we cannot blame others for our thoughts, words and deeds, and that if we do wrong it is up to us to do our best to rectify it.

★ We seek personal development.

There is much to learn in the world and in the Craft, but we do not expect others to feed us this information, we seek to expand our knowledge and extend our skills by personal effort. All Witches are aware that they will never know enough, let alone everything. This personal development also includes expanding our personal skills and attributes, 'ironing out' our personal misconceptions and problems, and working to become the best self we can. Witchcraft has been called 'a thinking person's belief system', and rightly so in my opinion, as it involves a course of personal exploration and general study which never ceases.

★ The Summerlands and reincarnation.

Witches believe that we live many lives and between them we return to the Summerlands, a resting-place where we review the lessons we have learned in the life we have just completed and select the lessons to be learned in the life to come. When we speak of reincarnation we do not mean that we come back as the same person but rather that our spirit is born again. Whilst it can be interesting to research previous incarnations, and the information we acquire may illuminate aspects of our current lives, it is necessary to remember that the personal responsibility we also believe in means that we cannot blame our past(s) for our current problems. We must live in the present and work towards achievement in this life.

★ We practise Herblore.

We utilize the properties of plants and nature for healing and self-improvement and in the course of our Magic. Herbs, plants and spices can be used in food and drink, lotions and ointments, sachets and talismans (Magical tokens), incense and candles. They can be used in their natural state (as I write this I have rosemary on my desk to aid my thoughts and concentration), fresh, dried or in the form of oil, as in aromatherapy, which has become so popular in recent years. The bulk of this book will be taken up with recipes and suggestions for the use of natural resources to enhance life.

 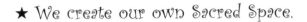
★ We create our own Sacred Space.

Witches do not have special buildings in which they worship, in fact most Witches do not even have a room or even a space set aside for working. They create their own working space wherever and whenever they need it, and this can be inside or out. This space is called the Circle and it is created in several steps. Briefly speaking, they are:

The invocation of the elements of Air, Fire, Water and Earth, which are the energies on which we draw. They are always called in this order as Air represents thought, which should precede all our actions. We bring the element of Spirit to the Circle ourselves and through the Divine.

The invitation of the Goddess and the God, the Divine, whose assistance we need to perform our working and in whose honour we gather.

The drawing of a Circle large enough to contain those taking part and the actions they are there to perform. This is usually done on the psychic level rather than on the physical, although some will place markers to show the boundary. The Circle is drawn clockwise (or Deosil) from the north-east point of the area, between Earth and Air, and overlaps at that point in order to ensure that it is complete. The Circle is there to contain the energy raised until it is ready to be released and to protect those within its boundaries from outside energies and distractions.

These steps can be formal and elaborate, as in group working, or very simple and performed using visualization when working on your own.

Any Craft-related action done within the Sacred Space will have more effect and potency than the same action performed outside the Sacred Space. Having said that, in most cases things can be made outside the Circle and then taken into it and blessed or consecrated for use. Alternatively, you can Magically enhance your remedies whilst making them and empower them for use.

Magically Enhancing and Empowering your Work

To Enhance Work in Preparation

Whether you are making a healing potion or bathing in preparation for a Magical working, the first step is to clear your mind of all distractions so that you can fully focus on your intent, for it is intent and focus which make the Magic work. One of the keys to this is to carefully prepare your working area. Make sure it is clean and tidy before you start, for physical distractions lead to mental ones.

You also have to carefully define your needs and goals. Make sure that you know what you intend to do and why. Are your motives pure? Having formulated your desire, you then need to assemble all your ingredients, checking that you have everything you need and finding substitutes where necessary. Then you can commence work.

Whilst working, you need to keep your goals firmly in mind, if necessary by writing them out and keeping a copy in front of you. You should also try to summon from within your-self the elements, in terms of thinking about what you are doing (Air), empowering it with enthusiasm (Fire) and emotion (Water), by the actual work (Earth) and by focusing your intent (Spirit). If you can, dedicate the work to a particular Goddess(es) and/or God(s), as you will find that they will lend their aid not only to your Magic, but also to making the physical side of things proceed more easily.

To Magically Empower a Product

There are many ways of empowering a potion or object, from simply placing it in the light of the Full Moon overnight to a full Ritual of Consecration (*see below*). However, you cannot sit food on the windowsill overnight for consumption the following day! Instead you might like to dedicate it to your chosen deity or deities. To do this, create a small clear space around your chosen item or product and visualize each of the elements in turn. See them in your mind's eye materializing over the product and then enhancing it with their energy. Then take up the item in your hands and call (either out loud, or in your mind) upon the Goddess and the God to lend their power to your intent. Visualize them reaching out and touching the item and blessing it. When you feel that this is complete, thank the Goddess and the God, and each of the elements, for their aid.

If you prefer a more formal approach, and you are creating something which does not have to be consumed immediately, then you can consecrate it ritually. This will involve setting an Altar and casting a Circle by invoking the elements of Air, Fire, Water and Earth, and inviting the Goddess and the God. After this, pass the object through the incense smoke and candle flame, then sprinkle it with water and salt whilst naming it and its purpose, and asking for their energy to enhance it. Next, you present it to the Goddess and the God and ask their blessing in the way described above. Lastly, you will need to remove the Circle and clear away your working space by thanking and banishing the elements and the Divine.

Disposing of your Spell

People often ask me how to dispose of spells, charms, sachets, and so on once they have fulfilled their purpose or the Magic is no longer required.

The first thing to do is to remember to give thanks to the Goddess and the God. It is not enough to just accept the Magic, you need to try to give back something too. Perhaps plant a useful herb in your garden or, if you have the space, a tree dedicated to the Gods. Alternatively, spend some time working on the land or clearing rubbish from your local park.

After you have given something back, then it is time to dispose of the sachet. Open it and scatter all the environmentally-friendly parts to the winds. Stones, crystals and charms should be buried or cast into the sea or a stream. The fabric of the sachet and any paper, perhaps with your intent written on, can be burned or torn into shreds and buried.

Keeping a Journal or Book of Shadows

In the Craft we often recommend that each Witch keeps their own Book of Shadows, so called because it is but a shadow of reality. In this they record their Magical workings and experiences, as well as their thoughts and feelings about the Craft. They use it to monitor their own progress and as a record for their future reference. In a Coven, the High Priestess may also ask to see this journal so that she may monitor the progress of those Witches in her care as well as help to guide their future development.

In herbal work it really is essential to keep a record of what you have done, how much of each ingredient you used, when and how you made it (including the phase of the Moon), when and how it was used, and the results. How else are you going to be able to monitor your progress and the efficacy of your products?

Whether you keep a formal Book of Shadows or a simple 'cookery' journal, it is important that you keep it safe from prying eyes, as even the thought that someone may be reading your thoughts is usually enough to stop you from recording them honestly (*see* p.204).

I would advise that starting such a journal is perhaps your first step on the road towards becoming a 'Kitchen Witch'.

Guidelines for Buying, Using and Storing Herbs and Plants

'Whenever ye have need of any thing...'

Many of the recipes in this book involve the use of herbs and plants whose uses and effects you may be unfamiliar with. So here are some guidelines to help you to use them safely and efficiently.

★ Buy what you need when you need it. A well-stocked herbalist's cupboard does not have to contain everything you may want one day, it only needs to contain what you are going to use. Probably the best way to start is by buying the ingredients you need for your first recipe and then adding to the store as you move from recipe to recipe.

★ Always store ingredients in clearly-labelled containers and take note of 'use by' dates. Many herbs quickly lose their potency; some can even become really quite unpleasant to taste as well. Almost every non-living ingredient will benefit from being kept in a cool dark place.

★ Plants should be kept in locations suitable to their needs, for example in or out of direct sunlight, and tended regularly. Many plants benefit from regular trimming, and if you don't intend to use them immediately you can dry and store the trimmings (labelled and dated) for future use. If you plant out herbs or other plants, keep a note of where they are, as many things die back over winter and it can be difficult to remember what and where they are after the resting season.

★ It is best not to take plants from the wild. You need to be absolutely certain that they are what you think they are, and nature often makes copies, which may be either harmful or useless for your purpose. You also have to be certain that plants are not endangered or protected; just because they are plentiful in your area does not mean that they are plentiful everywhere else. You need to be sure that they are not contaminated by 'fall-out' from car exhaust fumes, local chemicals or passing dogs! This may mean that you end up cultivating some unlikely species, such as dandelion, in your garden, but better that than using something which is not entirely safe.

★ Try to make things for immediate use, as this is when they are at their most potent. If you are making something to store for later, make sure you label it correctly and put a date on it. Even the best memory can fail from time to time.

★ Never eat or drink anything which is not designed for consumption unless you are 100 per cent certain what it is and are familiar with its possible effects. These days it is possible to buy most herbs from the supermarket or healthstore in packaging which makes it obvious whether you can ingest them or not. If you are buying by mail order, then check that your supplier is both knowledgeable and reputable, and don't be afraid to ask for their qualifications or for references. If you are buying living plants, get them from a reputable source which labels them carefully. In all cases try to obtain herbs which have been grown organically rather than those exposed to chemical fertilizers or pesticides.

★ Never give anything to anyone else without telling them what it contains. There will always be someone for whom it is inadvisable to take the most innocuous-sounding ingredient.

★ Do not give anything to pregnant women, babies or young children unless it is designed for their use. If you wish to give camomile to a baby to aid digestion, for example, look for a camomile drink designed for infants of the appropriate age. If in doubt, consult a doctor or pharmacist. Do not use aromatherapy oils, other than lavender, on pregnant women, nursing mothers, babies or children under 12 without consulting an experienced aromatherapist.

★ Any home-made lotions, soaps and creams should be tested on a small area of skin before use. You don't want to discover an allergy after you've covered your face with something! Quite often it is the base which can cause a reaction, so it is wise to test that before you put the effort into making a remedy. Do not expect home-made items to last anywhere near as long as their manufactured counterparts, as you will be neither filling them with preservatives nor boiling the life out of them. It is worth noting that many shop-bought preparations will have the scent of herbs rather than their active ingredients.

★ Experiment carefully and use your senses – smell and taste things cautiously. If something smells disgusting, it will probably taste pretty bad too. If it has green fur on it, it has probably gone off! If something seems to be disagreeing with you, stop using it. Herbal medicine should not have unpleasant side-effects.

★ In the case of illness, always seek conventional help as well. If it is something major, get a professional diagnosis and tell your practitioner what you intend to do to supplement their treatment. Some herbal remedies can conflict with modern medicines, especially the contraceptive pill. If you are sure your illness is minor, say, indigestion caused by overindulgence, by all means try a herbal remedy first, but if the symptoms persist, call on the professionals in case there is a more serious underlying complaint.

★ If using essential oils, make sure that they really are 100 per cent essential oils, not perfumed oils or blended oils. There are many cheap, and not so cheap, fakes on the market, so it is worth taking the extra time and effort to track down the real thing and pay the proper price for it. Perfume oils usually contain chemical scents and will not have the same effects as essential oils and some cheap ones can be positively damaging. Blended oils may contain almost anything in addition to what they own up to on the bottle, and in any case, once an oil has been blended, it will start to deteriorate much faster.

★ Always keep everything spotlessly clean – your hands, your preparation area, any bottles, pans or jars. However, try not to use large quantities of chemicals to clean and sterilize, particularly bleach, as this is quite toxic and will kill off the very properties of the plants you seek to use. Surfaces can be rubbed down with a salt and water paste then rinsed and dried carefully. Hands can be washed with ordinary soap and water, then dried. In both cases it is essential to make sure that the drying cloth is clean, as many of the germs in the kitchen are found on the tea towel! Containers should be of glass, not plastic, and after being thoroughly cleaned can be sterilized by completely immersing them in lightly-salted water and boiling them for ten minutes. As soon as they are cool enough to handle, allow them to dry naturally by standing them on their necks on a clean cloth. Do not eat, drink or smoke whilst making your preparations; the action of raising things to your mouth may contaminate your hands with germs.

Although the above instructions may look quite daunting at first glance, they are in fact the day-to-day practical precautions which we should take with anything we are going to consume or use on our bodies.

Working sensibly with herbs and plants is very rewarding, not only because of the cures that can be effected, but also because of the knowledge that we are in a position to help ourselves and those we care for. In addition, it is great fun.

Soaps and Bathing Preparations

'A proper person, properly prepared...'

An important part of any ritual is preparation, whether that be a Magical ritual or a daily one. For most people, a night out is preceded by a ritual of washing the body and hair, and often applying scents to set the mood. Whilst doing so they think about where they are going, what they will be doing and what they hope will happen. It is no different in the Craft; wherever possible we wash our bodies, or at least our hands, to remove not only the dirt of the day, but also the negative thoughts and feelings of day-to-day life. At the same time we also prepare our minds by thinking through what we are about to do and what we wish to achieve. Of course, this can be done with plain soaps and bathing products, but it can be greatly enhanced by the use of products which we have created, altered and Magically empowered. Here I am going to take a look at ways of creating or, more often, changing existing products to Magically enhance them.

Whilst it is possible to make soaps, bath foams, shampoos and anointing oils from first principles, it is not really practical for everyone. As a result I am going to talk mainly about how we can take existing products and change them for our purposes.

The use of such enhanced products does not have to be limited to preparation for ritual. Keeping a bar of healing or refreshing soap in the bathroom can help us through daily life. Preparing a bath foam to help encourage sleep can be invaluable for the parent of a young child who refuses to 'go down' at night. So, many of the following will not be set aside for Craft work, but will have a place in daily life.

Abbreviations

lb ★ pound
oz ★ ounce
fl oz ★ fluid ounce
tbsp ★ tablespoonful
(note this is not the same as a serving spoon), should be around 15 fl oz
tsp ★ teaspoonful, around 1/4 fl oz

Soaps

The basic ingredients for soap are in fact quite caustic, so it is not only easier but also more user-friendly to rework ready-made soap. The best kind to choose is a pure, unscented castille soap, although you can use this method with other kinds of unscented soaps.

First cut up (or grate) about 4 oz (1 cup) of the soap and place in a heatproof non-metallic container.

★ Add about ¼ cup (2 fl oz) of hot water and 1 tbsp of almond or apricot oil.

★ Leave until cool enough to handle and then mix in with your hands.
If the soap is floating on the water you will need to add more soap.

★ Leave for about ten minutes, mixing occasionally, by which time the
soap should be soft and mushy. If it is not, place the bowl into a saucepan
of boiling water and heat gently.

★ When the soap, water and oil are completely blended, add any dry ingredients.

★ When the mixture is cool, add any essential oils. It is important that the
mixture be cool as essential oils evaporate quickly in heat. Note that essential
oils should be added until they overcome the original odour of the soap,
so how much will depend on the type of soap and oil you use.

★ Blend really thoroughly and divide the mixture into four to six pieces,
depending on the size of the soaps you finally require.

★ Now squeeze these soaps, removing as much excess water as possible,
into the shape you require – balls, ovals or whatever – and tie in cheesecloth.

★ Hang in a warm dry place until completely hard.

The soaps can then be used or wrapped in cheesecloth and kept or given away. As an aside, ordinary soap will always last longer if you take it out of its wrapper and keep it in a warm dry place to get completely hard before use.

All the following recipes are based on the above quantity of soap. As people relate to different scents in different ways, these can be adjusted according to your own preferences. Additionally, you can adapt any of the following to a plain unscented liquid soap, but do be aware that liquid soaps are usually detergent-based and hence not really very good for the skin. Where it says 'oil' in the following recipes I refer to essential oil, except in the case of the coconut oil in the dry skin recipe. When using herbs or other dried ingredients, make sure that you remove the really hard woody bits to make the soap pleasant to use. If you do not like textured or 'gritty' soap, then substitute drops of the appropriate oils.

It is worth noting that when using soap you should always lather it in your hands and then wash the rest of yourself with the lather. It is not a good idea to rub any soap directly onto other areas of the skin as it can be too harsh and drying.

Mental and Physical Cleansing

This is excellent for use before any ritual, or indeed any time when you need to mark the division between one part of your day and another, for example the transition from your work self to your home self.

1 tbsp lavender flowers
6 drops frankincense oil
6 drops sandalwood oil
4 drops jasmine oil

Esbat Soap

This takes the cleansing recipe a step further in that it is designed to prepare you for the working element of ritual and Magic, when you will need the additional ability to focus and control.

1 tbsp rosemary leaves
1/2 tsp ground cinnamon
6 drops frankincense oil
6 drops sandalwood oil
4 drops jasmine oil
4 drops oil of orange
(you can literally scrape the oil from the outside of an orange using a blunt knife)

Sabbat Soap

The Sabbats are less a time of working and more a time of celebration, hence a different blend. Of course you could make different soaps for different Sabbats, altering the ingredients to match the key points of the festival and the season, in which case you might wish to make a smaller quantity of soap and use it on a daily basis for the seven days prior to the Sabbat, in preparation for it.

1 tbsp rosemary leaves
½ tbsp jasmine flowers
6 drops sandalwood oil
6 drops frankincense oil
3 drops cinnamon oil

Divination

If you are learning divination, perhaps by reading the Tarot, or do this on a regular basis, then it is worth having a soap especially for the purpose.

6 drops myrrh oil
6 drops frankincense oil
4 drops bay oil
***(or take 10 crushed bay leaves, cover with 2 tbsp boiling water and leave for
several days before using this liquid as the water in your recipe)***

Driving Away Negative Thoughts and Feelings

There are times when we all suffer from self-doubt or a lack of self-esteem or when it seems that everything is working out badly. This is an excellent soap for bringing the spirit back into balance, especially if used in conjunction with other uplifting recipes in this book.

6 drops frankincense oil
6 drops sandalwood oil
2 tsp jasmine flowers
4 drops jasmine oil
4 drops neroli oil
4 drops ylang ylang oil
2 drops ginger oil
4 drops rose oil
(optional as many people find it makes the scent too cloying)

All-Purpose Healing

Lavender is the all-purpose healer and works on mind, body and spirit. Living with a fairly standard accident-prone toddler I use this (or slight variants) as the daily soap in the home.

1 tablespoon lavender flowers (*fresh if possible*)
6 drops lavender oil

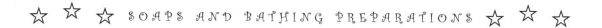
Antiseptic

This soap is good at combating infections, particularly of the skin, and is also helpful in healing general cuts and grazes.

1 tablespoon honey
1 tablespoon thyme
4 drops tea tree oil
2 drops myrrh oil

Refreshing and Mentally Stimulating

This is especially good for studying or preparing for exams, or any time when you have a need of mental stimulus, as it helps the mind to focus and aids the memory.

$\frac{1}{2}$ tablespoon chopped fresh rosemary leaves
**(*dried can be used, but they should be added with the hot water at*
the start of the process so that they have time to soften)**
$\frac{1}{2}$ tablespoon dried basil
6 drops rosemary oil
6 drops grapefruit oil
4 drops pine oil
4 drops peppermint oil

For Dry Skin

Dry skin generally benefits from not coming into contact with any kind of soap or detergent and I recommend washing in tepid water only. However, there will be times when soap is desirable, hence the following recipe. Instead of almond oil in the basic recipe, use coconut oil.

1 tablespoon rolled oats
6 drops geranium oil
6 drops sandalwood oil
4 drops lavender oil
2 to 4 drops patchouli oil or rose oil
(add the latter slowly as these are highly scented and not to everyone's taste)

Insect Repellent

Whilst I usually recommend using no scent at all as the best way to avoid insect bites, I have also had good results with this recipe.

10–20 drops lemongrass oil
5 drops lavender oil

If you are not going to expose your skin to sunlight, you can also add 5 drops bergamot oil, but do be aware that it can make some skins photosensitive and has been linked to skin cancer when combined with exposure to the sun.

Bath Foams and Oils

Whilst soaps are excellent, there are times when you want to wash with something for a special purpose but do not intend to use that product day in and day out, or even for weeks at a time. In such cases it is easier to make a small quantity of bath foam or oil for the purpose. For your base you can use any unscented bath foam or oil. Many people choose those intended for babies, although they do have quite a strong fragrance of their own. My personal favourite base is the plain foaming bath oil from The Body Shop, as it has oil in the blend and therefore takes up essential oils quite well, but it is not all oil and so does not leave you with a greasy ring around the bath.

Whatever your choice of base, there are two routes you can go down. One is to make up a quantity of your recipe and store it in a well-labelled glass bottle in a cool dark place between uses. The other is to make just enough for the one bath immediately prior to use. The following recipes are based on the one-bath recipe, using about a tablespoonful of your base foam or a teaspoonful of oil, so you will need to multiply up the ingredients if you are making a larger quantity.

When using essential oils in the bath you should make sure that the bathwater is not too hot – not only does this release the fragrance of the oils too quickly, but it can also be quite debilitating. Try to make your bathtime a relaxing event – don't rush and hurry, and whilst in the water spend time focusing on what you are about to do. Try bathing by candlelight – it is an excellent way of setting a mood.

Preparing for Magical Work

Use the time in the bath first to soak away the cares of the day and secondly to focus on the Magical work you are about to commence.

2 drops frankincense oil
2 drops sandalwood oil
1 drop orange oil

Divination Bath

Before undertaking any kind of divination, or to promote prophetic dreams, have a long soak in this formula. It is best to do this by candlelight and not to use a base oil or foam or any other scented products (such as soap).

Take 2 crushed bay leaves and 1 tablespoonful of thyme, add to 1 pint of very hot water and leave to stand for an hour. Strain this liquid and add to your bath with:

5 drops lemongrass oil
2 drops myrrh oil

To Promote a Good Night's Sleep

This is an excellent bath to take just before bed and is also suitable for children over the age of two (for those under two, omit the valerian). Don't use it every night, as you can easily become accustomed to the effects and find that it doesn't work when you really need it.

6 drops lavender oil
2 drops valerian oil (1 *drop for children over two years*)

Colds and Flu

As soon as you feel the onset of a cold, have a long relaxing soak in the following:

4 drops lavender oil
2 drops eucalyptus oil
2 drops jasmine oil
1 drop cinnamon oil
1 drop ginger oil

After bathing, wrap up warmly and go to bed with a warm drink.

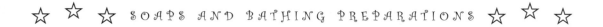

Wake-Up Bath

This is excellent for those mornings when you feel sluggish or have a busy day ahead or even for the morning after the night before. Try to have the bath quite cool and stay in the water for at least 10 minutes to let the oils take effect.

3 drops rose oil
3 drops rosemary oil
3 drops rosewood oil

After Exercise

When you have exerted yourself and feel that you should ward off muscular aches and pains, try this one:

3 drops lavender oil
3 drops camomile oil
2 drops lemongrass oil
2 drops rosemary oil

Romance Bath

When preparing for a romantic encounter, whether out on a date or at home with a loved one, soak yourself in the following:

2 drops sandalwood oil
2 drops jasmine oil
1 drop neroli oil
1 drop ylang ylang oil

If you really want to add spice to the encounter, add 1 drop of cardamom oil, but be prepared for the results!

Self-Care Bath

We all have times in our lives when we need to care for our own physical, mental and emotional state. In fact most of us neglect ourselves in these respects far too often. But if you do not look after yourself, how are you going to do the best for those you care for? Take time out at least once a week to treat yourself. Make the environment as pleasant as you can – perhaps light candles around the bath and play some soothing music. Above all, turn off the phone and lock the door to make sure you are not disturbed even by your near and dear. Then relax in the following:

2 drops frankincense oil
2 drops jasmine oil
2 drops sandalwood oil
2 drops ylang ylang oil
1 drop rose oil
1 drop ginger oil

Stress Relief Bath

This is for those times when the world really has been getting on top of you and you feel really stressed out!

8 drops neroli oil
4 drops clary sage oil
4 drops lavender oil
2 drops cedarwood oil

'Bath Teas'

There is another way of adding herbs to your bath and that is to make them into a 'tea'. You will need to steep the herbs in a small amount of boiling water for around 15 to 20 minutes and then strain the resultant liquid into your bath. You can of course add the herbs to the water directly, but then you will have the problem of getting all the bits off your skin and the sides of the bath!

If you prefer to shower with any of these preparations then it is best to tie the herbs into a face cloth (wash cloth) or piece of fabric and rub it directly into the skin after washing but before your final rinse.

Magical Working

3 tsp rosemary
3 tsp jasmine petals
a pinch of ginger
a pinch of cinnamon
grated peel of half an orange
(try to ensure that you don't get any of the white pith into the mixture)

Divination

3 tsp thyme
2 tsp rose petals
1 tsp sage
a pinch of nutmeg
grated peel of a lemon

To Remove Negative Influences

In addition to the herbs, some people also recommend placing a clear quartz crystal into the bath to absorb any negative influences. Make sure you remove this before pulling the plug, so as not to lose it, and then rinse it under cold running water for 10 minutes to cleanse it.

4 tsp rosemary
2 tsp lavender
1 tsp crushed juniper berries
4 crushed bay leaves
1 tsp salt

Self-Control Bath

For use when trying to break old habits or when going on a diet.

2 tsp rosemary
2 tsp fennel
1 tsp sage
1 tsp lavender

Healing Bath

4 tsp lavender
2 tsp rosemary
2 tsp rose petals
1 tsp salt

This is especially helpful after childbirth, in which case the salt should be increased to 1 tbsp, but then it is not useful for showering.

Easing Coughs and Colds

4 tsp lavender
4 tsp rosemary
4 crushed cloves

You can also add a couple of drops of eucalyptus oil to the water.

Beauty Bath

Place a piece of amber in the bathwater (making sure you retrieve it before pulling the plug) and whilst bathing visualize yourself growing in beauty. Focus on your positive points; try not to think of any negatives at all. It is said that wearing amber also enhances beauty.

3 tsp lavender
3 tsp rose petals
2 tsp rosemary
2 tsp jasmine flowers

Of course you do not have to limit yourself to the recipes given here. Using herbs, flowers and essential oils you can create any number of your own bathing preparations. The secret to successfully creating your own recipes is to take your time in experimenting. Make sure you are relaxed, take a herb and smell it. What does it remind you of? How does it make you feel? Is it uplifting or relaxing? Does it remind you of spring, summer, autumn or winter? If it is edible, taste it and ask yourself the same questions. Secondly, keep a record of your experiments. If, after using a blend, you find you have vivid dreams, then make a note of it. Remember that everyone can react differently to different plants or blends. If a blend intended to give a good night's rest makes you feel alert and ready to take on the world, then that is how it works for you. Above all, have fun with it.

Oils, Lotions and Potions

'Here I charge you in this sign...'

From earliest times people have used oils to soften the skin, to perfume themselves, to heal and to enhance Magical workings. Some ancient civilizations rarely used soap in any form, preferring to apply oil and then scrape it from the skin, removing not only dirt but also loose dead skin. These days many of us find oil too greasy and prefer to use creams and lotions on a daily basis. However, creams, whether solid or liquid, are simply a way of suspending oil and water in a user-friendly way. To do this effectively other ingredients are added which stop the blend separating out or going off. Whilst it is possible to make your own creams and lotions, blending lanolin, animal fat and water, it is far simpler to start with an unscented lotion or cream which has been mass produced.

The main practical difference between a lotion, cream or oil is in how you intend to use it. If the area to be covered is large, then you will want a lotion, which can be easily spread and is relatively rapidly absorbed. If you are treating a small area or one which requires a level of massage, perhaps a bruise or a sore joint, then a cream may be more practical, being thicker and more slowly absorbed. There is also the matter of preference. For some any cream is too thick, for others a lotion simply does not suit the skin. Oils can be added to baths, as outlined in the preceding chapter, and whilst you may notice that some of the following recipes are similar, you will also notice some differences. This is because these are intended for direct contact with the skin, rather than the larger dilutions you get in a bath or when using soap. They are Magically no less effective, they are just safer to use undiluted.

Magical application is somewhat different as in this case you want the essence of the ingredients rather than the effects of the base. Additionally many of the following oils need not simply be used on the skin but may be applied to a candle or talisman in the course of Magic or ritual. You can also choose to use the recipe in an oil burner, although you may wish to scale down the quantities and add them direct to the water in the burner.

The following recipes are designed to be used with 3 tbsp of cream, lotion or of base oil. Choose a cream or lotion which is unscented or carries very little obvious perfume and which suits your skin and your pocket. My favourite base lotion is a cheap unscented general purpose handcream which I've been using all over very successfully for years. For a cream to be used medicinally I often favour petroleum jelly.

When it comes to selecting a base oil for anointing and Magical work, again choose one which suits your skin and purse. If you can, try out sweet almond, avocado, wheatgerm, apricot kernel and jojoba. Even olive oil works for some people. Select the one you prefer; contrary to the statements of many practitioners, as long as you buy from a reputable source, the oils and your Magical intentions will overcome any so called 'impurities' in the cheaper varieties. Often is it worth enquiring at your pharmacy, rather than a New Age or specialist supplier, who may charge more.

When using the following recipes please remember not to use aromatherapy oils, other than lavender, on pregnant women, nursing mothers, babies or children under 12 without consulting an experienced aromatherapist.

Esbat Oil

This is for personal anointing before any Full Moon ritual. It would not usually be used on any candle or object for Magical intent, as either a specially prepared oil or an empowering oil would be used instead.

2 drops frankincense
2 drops rosemary
1 drop jasmine
1 drop sandalwood

Sabbat Oil

An oil for personal anointing before any of the eight Sabbats, this can also be used to anoint the Altar candle at a Sabbat celebration.

3 drops frankincense
2 drops myrrh
2 drops sandalwood
1 drop cinnamon

Goddess Oil

Wear this to honour the Goddess or apply it to a candle to invoke her assistance.

2 drops jasmine oil
2 drops myrrh oil
1 drop rose oil

God Oil

Wear this to honour the God or apply it to a candle to invite his strength.

2 drops sandalwood oil
2 drops orange oil
1 drop cinnamon oil

Power Oil

Use this to enhance or empower any Magical working.

4 drops orange oil
1 drop cinnamon oil
1 drop ginger oil
1 drop pine oil

Divination Oil

Anoint yourself and/or use this in an oil burner before any acts of divination.

2 drops frankincense oil
2 drops lemongrass oil
2 drops nutmeg oil
2 drops clary sage oil
1 drop bay oil
1 drop rose oil

Communication Oil

Use this whenever you want to facilitate communication, perhaps a job interview or difficult meeting. If the situation affects you, wear the oil, if it affects another, use it on a talisman (Magical token) or on your Magical candle.

4 drops rosemary oil
2 drops sandalwood oil
2 drops jasmine oil
2 drops ylang ylang oil
1 drop cedarwood oil

Banishing Oil

Use this to drive away negative thoughts, feelings and influences. If you feel that the influences are coming from outside, you can put a few drops of this over each window and doorway to your home. Otherwise wear it personally or use it Magically on a candle.

4 drops frankincense oil
2 drops bergamot oil
2 drops clary sage oil
2 drops lavender oil

Wealth Oil

This oil will not simply bring you money – Magically speaking, that is very dangerous. It will, however, increase your opportunities to earn money.

3 drops basil oil
2 drops ginger oil
1 drop vanilla essence or extract (*not flavouring*)

Sleep Oil

This oil will aid restful sleep and, with the addition of 2 drops of clary sage, enhance dreams.

6 drops lavender oil
3 drops frankincense oil
1 drop valerian oil

Study Oil

Anoint yourself with this before and during periods of study, also before exams or other tests of memory. This blend can also be used in a burner whilst working or studying.

4 drops rosemary oil
4 drops basil oil
2 drops grapefruit oil
1 drop cajuput oil (*optional*)

General Healing

This is an all-purpose blend which can be incorporated into 2 tbsp of any base and applied direct to the skin.

6 drops lavender oil
2 drops frankincense oil
2 drops myrrh oil
2 drops jasmine oil

Muscular Aches and Pains

Where there is muscular pain it is best to massage the oil gently into the skin. Unless you are qualified, it is a good idea to avoid attempting any deep massage involving the muscles themselves.

4 drops lavender oil
2 drops rosemary oil
2 drops marjoram oil
2 drops cypress oil
2 drops black pepper oil

Pain in the Joints

As with the preceding blend, the lotion or cream should be gently massaged into the skin, but no manipulation of the underlying tissues should be attempted. If possible, the affected area should be covered (not bound), for about half an hour after treatment.

4 drops lavender oil
3 drops camomile oil
2 drops black pepper oil
2 drops juniper oil

Digestive Complaints

Whilst you may think it unlikely that anything you put on your skin will help your digestion, you could well be surprised. Try:

4 drops lavender oil
3 drops peppermint oil
2 drops fennel oil
2 drops rosemary oil

Colds and Flu

If you're suffering from either of these, you really should be in bed, but I know that that's not always possible, so the following might help you get through the day. Place a few drops on a tissue and inhale at regular intervals.

4 drops lavender oil
2 drops cinnamon oil
2 drops eucalyptus oil
2 drops jasmine oil
2 drops cypress oil
1 drop ginger oil

For children under the age of three I recommend simply putting the lavender, eucalyptus and jasmine oils on a tissue and placing this near them but out of their reach.

Emotional Balancing

Use this in a burner, on a tissue or to anoint yourself whenever you have emotional swings or thoughts and feelings seem to be getting out of hand.

4 drops geranium oil
4 drops lavender oil
2 drops grapefruit oil
1 drop bergamot oil
1 drop fennel oil

Exhaustion and Overwork

If you are exhausted, the first step to healing is to get enough rest, and for this the above Sleep Oil is excellent. However, if you have been through a prolonged period of overwork you may also like to use this uplifting blend to carry you through after resting.

3 drops basil oil
2 drops lavender oil
2 drops clary sage oil
2 drops lemongrass oil

Self-Confidence

Use this when your confidence needs a boost or when you need to impress someone, perhaps at an interview. Do not use too much of this oil, however – the idea is for it to work on the subconscious level, not for people to be able to detect the scent.

3 drops bergamot oil
2 drops jasmine oil
2 drops ylang ylang oil
2 drops neroli oil

Sadness and Regret

Sometimes we all look back and wish we had done things differently. Whilst this oil helps to alleviate these feelings, in the Craft we believe that true healing will not come until you have also done what you can to put things right again.

2 drops bergamot oil
2 drops rose oil
2 drops benzoin oil
2 drops jasmine oil
2 drops hyssop oil

A Gathering of Friends

Use this to promote feelings of warmth, friendship and relaxation whenever friends gather. Anoint yourself, and anyone else who feels they would like to share in it, or use it in an oil burner.

2 drops frankincense oil
2 drops jasmine oil
2 drops clary sage oil
1 drop cardamom oil

The Magical Application of Oils

Whilst essential oils all have their own healing properties, these can be Magically enhanced by invoking the Goddess and the God and the elements as well as focusing on your intent (*see* Chapter 1, 'Witchcraft, and Empowering your Herbal Work'). However, when using them in a Magical context, such as anointing yourself or an object, there are also ways in which you can again increase their effectiveness.

Anointing the Self

There are certain parts of the body which are more receptive to anointing oils than others – it is not simply a question of dabbing on the oil as you would a perfume. These places include the temples, third eye (the point between your eyes just over the brow bone) and the chakra points, depending on your intent. For general purposes you can use the wrists, but not the sides of the neck or behind the ears. Anointing can take place on its own or as a Rite in itself. As with everything in the Craft, the important thing is to be clear about your intent and to focus properly.

A Self-Blessing

The Rite of Self-Blessing is probably the best way to apply any oil for Magical purposes. First ensure that you have a few undisturbed minutes and your prepared oil is to hand. Now centre yourself, put aside any intrusive thoughts from your daily life and think about what you intend to achieve. Close your eyes and visualize the Goddess or the God (whichever you feel is most appropriate for your working) with you. Now say the following:

'Bless me, Mother [or "Father" in the case of the God], for I am your child.

Blessed be my feet that shall walk in your path.
(**Anoint each foot with a single drop of oil.**)

Blessed be my knees that shall kneel at the Sacred Altar.
(**Anoint each knee with a single drop of oil.**)

Blessed be my womb ("loins" for a man) which bringest forth the life of man.
(**Anoint your belly just above the pubic bone.**)

Blessed be my breast, formed in strength and beauty. (**Anoint your breasts.**)

Blessed be my lips that shall utter thy names.
(**Anoint yourself with a single drop just above your top lip.**)

Blessed be my nose that shall breathe the Sacred essence.
(**Anoint the bridge of your nose.**)

Blessed be my eyes that shall see thy way.
(**Anoint each closed eyelid, keeping the oil well away from your eyes.**)

Bless me, Mother, for I am thy child.' (**Anoint your third eye.**)

Now remain where you are for a few minutes and visualize the Goddess or God holding you in their arms in a loving blessing.

When you are ready, put your oil safely away and go about your intent.

Note that the oil you anoint yourself with should be more like a barely perceptible smear, not a rivulet. More oil is not more effective, but it will increase the chances of you getting some into your eyes or mouth, which could be quite uncomfortable.

A less formal way of performing this, should you be in non-sympathetic company, is to visualize yourself going through this Rite but simply anoint your third eye.

Using a Lotion or Cream on Another Person

If your subject is sympathetic to the Craft or to alternate forms of healing, then you will be able to work quite openly with them. In this case gentle massage is probably the best way to deliver your blend. If they have a specific part of the body which is causing trouble, such as an ankle or wrist, then you can work directly on that part. If however, their malaise is more general, perhaps a cold or stress, then you can massage the shoulders, hands or feet, or whatever they and you feel comfortable with.

Whilst gently massaging the lotion into the skin, take care not to interact with the underlying tissues unless you are a qualified masseuse. Visualize the ingredients in the oil working their way into the person's body and the aromas seeping into their spirit. Visualize these driving out all negative influences and leaving a warm golden healing light.

When you have finished, make sure that you wash your hands thoroughly, not only to remove the oils but also to wash away any negativity that you may have accumulated in the course of the healing.

Anointing a Candle or Other Object

Many people like to burn a candle to focus their Magical intent and to 'send the Magic on its way'. You can use a candle you have made for the purpose or buy one of the colour which you feel is most appropriate (*see* Chapter 5, 'Candles and Incenses').

To anoint a candle, hold it horizontally in front of you. With your forefinger place one or two drops of oil in the centre and, using both hands, spread the oil from the centre to the ends whilst visualizing your goals. When you are certain the candle is covered, but not dripping, with oil, place it in a holder and light it. Spend a moment or two visualizing the power of the Magic taking hold and moving out to its destination.

Ideally the candle should be allowed to burn all the way down, but as you must *never* leave a burning candle unattended, it is permissible to extinguish it and relight it at a later point. However, this should only be done for the same intent and should take place within three days (at most) of the starting of the Magic.

Other objects can be anointed, for example a talisman, in which case a small drop of oil should be placed on each side or face of the object whilst visualizing your goal. The talisman should then either be put straight into use or wrapped carefully and put away until it can be given to the recipient.

Using an Oil Burner

Here you will be releasing the fragrance and energy of the oils into the atmosphere via the warmed water in the burner, so it is important that your burner will hold enough water to make this effective. There are many expensive and decorative burners which barely hold a tablespoonful of water. You would be far better off with a cheap one with a large 'well'.

Alternatively, you can make your own from two clean empty tin cans. Both cans should have the lids removed so as to minimize the sharp edges left at the top, the lower can needs to have a number of holes punched into the side (a skewer will usually do this) and the upper can or 'well' needs to sit comfortably on top. Place water in the well and your nightlite in the lower can, put it on a heatproof surface and you have a home-made oil burner.

Once you have your burner, light the candle and allow the water to start warming before adding your oil. As you add the oil, visualize the vapours reaching out and pervading everything until they reach your Magical goal. Visualize that goal being achieved, then sit back and enjoy the scent you have created.

Again, the candle should not be allowed to burn unattended; indeed, it is a good idea not only to put it out but also to make sure that the surface under your burner is not hot before you leave it.

If you also burn perfume oils, it is worth having two oil burners, with one reserved for Magical purposes. Essential oils are highly volatile and most are easily removed from the well, whereas perfume oils are not and often leave a sticky residue which may contaminate future workings.

Candles and Incenses

'Earth and Water, Air and Fire...'

 Not everything made in the Witches' kitchen is necessarily food or drink. Some Witches also make their own candles and incenses. These are superior to most shop-bought ones, not only because they can be tailor-made for the occasion or purpose, but also because they are made with focus and intent, hence the Magic starts even before they are actually used. Candles and incense are integral parts of Magical work. Candles are lit to create the Sacred Space and are burned to set Magic in motion. Incense also creates the ritual mood, as well as mentally preparing you for the work you intend to do.

Candle-Making

Making your own candles is great fun, but does need a certain amount of preparation. You really do need to have separate pans to heat your wax in, otherwise you risk leaving a taint on your cooking utensils, but you can always buy second-hand ones. You will also need to get hold of the raw ingredients – wax, stearin, wax colour, wicks and mould seal – as well as the moulds in which they set. In addition you will need, at least until you are very skilled, a huge amount of old newspaper with which to cover everything in case of spillage.

Probably the easiest way to start your candle-making is to buy a kit. These are sold in art and craft shops and in the toy section of many stores. They have the advantage of supplying all the ingredients you need together with some easy-to-follow instructions. If your kit suggests you need a wax thermometer, you can ignore this advice, so long as you are prepared to watch your wax like a hawk all the time it is being heated! Even with a thermometer, you cannot afford to leave molten or heating wax unattended. Once you have a kit and have started making candles with the ingredients supplied, then you can buy additional ingredients as and when you need them and also move on to buying specialist moulds, or even making your own.

Basic Candle-Making

The basic ingredients are wax, stearin, wick, wax colour, moulds and mould seal:

★ Wax is usually sold in powder or pellet form. Of course you can also melt down the odds and ends of candles you have burned, although be careful when mixing colours and scents. Do not recycle candle ends which have been used for Magic (you should have burned them down anyway) into new candles for Magical purposes, or you may end up with very confused Magic!

★ Stearin, which helps the candle to burn slowly and evenly and prevents dripping, usually comes as a powder. It should be added to wax in the ratio of roughly 1 part stearin to 6 parts wax.

★ Wicks are sold in a variety of sizes and it is important to use the right size, otherwise your candle will either burn too quickly (wick too big) or the melting wax will flood the wick and put it out (wick too small).

★ Mould seal is used to make an airtight seal at the top of the mould, which will be the bottom when you add the molten wax. You can also use chewing gum or plasticine. Do not use Blu-tac, as it will melt!

To these raw ingredients you can add colour, scent and anything you want to include in the candle. Colour is sold as dye discs, or you can use wax crayons. Whilst a huge range of colours are available you can pretty much make any colour you like using red, yellow and blue, varying shades by adding more or less colour. However, black is a useful addition to this, as it is not really possible to blend black without using a huge amount of colouring agent. To perfume your candle you can use perfume oil or essential oil if you are intending a Magical purpose. Other additions can include a pinch of herbs (not too much or you risk having a bonfire when you light the candle), a gemstone or even an attractive pebble. Do not add quantities of anything that will burn when the flame reaches it. There has been a series of candles on the market with plastic flowers buried in the wax – I shudder to think what happens if they catch light!

When making candles, clear a work surface close to your cooker, as you do not want to be walking around with a lot of molten wax. Also, make sure that no small children or animals are present. Whilst the wax should not be allowed to reach a temperature where it will seriously burn, wax spills do hurt and you do not want to take any chances.

Next, cover the area and the floor with newspaper. Even the most skilled candle-maker can have an accident and it is very tedious to have to clear up molten wax, which can also stain if it is highly coloured.

As molten wax is highly flammable, making candles is an activity which requires your full attention. Only heat wax while supervising it directly. Once it has melted, use it, don't leave it over the heat. It is simple enough to remelt it if you require some for topping up. Do not wander off to take a phone call or answer the door without first removing any melting wax from the heat.

If you do have the misfortune to set fire to your melting wax, smother the flames with a damp towel. Never pour water on it, as it will react like a chip-pan or fat fire.

Mix the wax and stearin, place into a heatproof container and place that in turn into a saucepan of water. Warm it up gently, adding colour if you are using it. While the wax is melting, get out all your other ingredients, moulds, etc.

As soon as you have some melted wax you can prime the wicks. This means dipping them briefly in a little melted wax. It helps when threading the wicks into the moulds, if you are using them.

Once all the wax is melted it is ready for making candles (for various techniques, see below). Try to ensure that it remains at a steady temperature. If you are adding scent or anything else, this should be done just before you pour the wax.

If you are using moulds, once you have filled a mould you will need to tap the sides to remove any air bubbles. Moulded candles also need to be topped up during the setting process, otherwise you may get a huge dent in the bottom. To increase the speed of setting you may want to have a bowl of cold water into which you can stand your finished candles. I also find that moulded candles can be 'encouraged' by placing them in the fridge. It makes them easier to release from the moulds too.

When the candles are fully set they can be released from the moulds and the ends of the wicks trimmed ready for use. For a professional finish, dip the candle in melted wax, without stearin, to give a glaze.

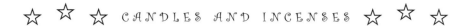
Types of Candle

Moulded Candles

Probably the easiest way to make candles is using purpose-built moulds. These come in two main varieties; rubber or rigid plastic. Rubber moulds have to be peeled off the finished candles, a process which requires quite a bit of skill. Also, you cannot use stearin in rubber moulds as it rots the mould, hence the finished candles will burn rapidly and almost certainly drip (or run). Solid moulds are easier to use and can also be improvised from other items.

To use a solid mould:

★ First ensure that your chosen vessel is heatproof.

★ Next, check that you will be able to remove your finished candle. Place your mould open end down on a flat surface. It should not be wider at the top than the bottom and the bottom should be wide enough to allow you to pour the wax in safely. At the top you will need a hole large enough for you to thread the wick through. Note that when making the candle you will need to turn the mould the other way up and will need to find some way of making sure it is stable on its narrower end. I usually find that I can prop it up in a cup or bowl.

★ Thread your wick through the narrow end and secure with a small stick (a used match is perfect), and seal the opening.

★ Tie the other end of the wick to an object large enough to be balanced over the wide end of the mould (bamboo skewers are ideal) and ensure that the wick is tight.

★ Pour the molten wax in and allow it to set. You will need to top it up from time to time otherwise you will be left with a dent in the base of your candle.

A quicker variation on this is to fill the mould with unmelted wax pellets and top it up with strongly-coloured molten wax, which gives a mottled or marbled effect. This technique can be used to make candles which contain a gemstone, perhaps related to a person's birthsign. Corresponding the colour of the candle, the scent you have added and a small gemstone bedded about one third of the way into the wax makes these into rather special 'healing' candles (see below).

Alternatively, you can place chunks of coloured wax in the mould and top it up with uncoloured or lightly coloured wax. This is a great way of using up odd scraps of candle, but you must remove all the old bits of wick.

Dipped Candles

Dipping is the technique used to make tall thin candles, often called dining candles. Dipped candles are usually made in pairs.

Take a length of wick a little over twice the length of candles you intend to make, loop it over a piece of dowel (or use a wooden spoon handle) and dip it into the melted wax repeatedly to build up layers of wax, until your candles are the thickness you require.

Dipping is a time-consuming process, as it is essential to proceed slowly, allowing each layer of wax to set before the next dip. You can dip the candles into cold water after each wax dip, but you must be certain that no drop of water remains on them before putting them back in the molten wax, as this can cause spattering. Also each dip has to be accomplished rapidly, otherwise the molten wax will simply melt the wax already on the wick. For this reason your wax should be only just molten – look for the beginnings of setting at the edges of your container. A further complication is the attraction the two candles will have for each other – and once they are welded together, there is little you can do to part them!

Once the basic candle shape has been achieved, dipping into a succession of coloured waxes, immersing the candles a little less deeply each time, can produce striped candles. Another variation is to take white candles and dip them into strong-coloured wax. However, this is not suitable for Magical purposes, as those candles really should be of a solid colour.

Rolled Candles

These are made from sheets of beeswax and, as the name suggests, rolled around the wick (which will need to be secured with a little melted wax). They are to all intents and purposes made cold, as the wax does not have to be melted. However, beeswax sheets are not cheap, or for that matter easy to obtain. Also, pure beeswax candles do not contain stearin, so will burn very quickly and are likely to drip.

Sand Candles

These are great fun, but can be messy to make.

★ You will need some fine sand (ask a local builder for half a bucketful). Make sure the sand is clean, putting it through a sieve if necessary.

★ Place the sand in a wide container, dampen it and press it down very thoroughly.

★ Press an object (plant pot, tin can or even an ornament) firmly down into the sand to make an impression. Note that sand will not give detailed or delicate shapes.

★ Now tie a length of wick to a small heavy object – a stone with a hole in it (often called a Witch stone) is very appropriate, but a heavy nut or washer will do.

★ Press your stone into the centre of the impression in the sand and tie the other end of the wick to a stick which is balanced across the top of your container. Try to ensure the wick is tight.

★ Now gently pour in the molten wax, remembering to top it up as it sets.
★ When the candle is completely hard, take it out of the container and brush all the loose sand off. I prefer to do this outside.

★ Remove the excess wick from the base and cut off the weight, leaving enough wick to light.

★ Take a sharp knife and carve a pattern into the sides of your candle
so that the light will shine though as the candle burns.

Decorating Finished Candles

Candles can be decorated in a number of ways. In most cases this should be done before overdipping in plain wax. You might like to try the following:

★ Dip a candle several times in a contrasting colour wax, then carve into the
top surface to reveal the underlying colour.

★ Paint pictures or patterns onto a finished candle with some contrasting wax
or with paint mixed with water and washing up liquid to produce a paste.

★ Make a stencil and dab the paint on with a sponge.

★ Take pressed flowers and stick them to the candle with a little molten wax.
Press down with a heated metal spoon and redip quickly in plain melted wax.

Choosing Colours and Scents for your Purpose

Candles for Magical purposes should be of solid colour, or colours, not simply white ones overdipped in another colour. Also scents should be essential oils, or scents made from pure ingredients, not simply perfumes added to the mix (although overdipping and perfumes are fine if your candles are simply intended to be decorative).

All colours and scents have what are called correspondences. These are things to which they are linked, either traditionally or because you consider them to be significant. If you are working Magic for a friend, for example, you might choose a colour which represents their birthsign, but you might prefer to choose a colour which you know to be their favourite instead. The former would be a traditional correspondence, the latter the correspondence you have chosen. You do not need to work only with birthsigns, you can choose colours and scents which reflect your purpose or some other aspect of your working. Also, it is more important for the Magic to actually take place rather than to wait for some obscure ingredient to turn up, so you may find that you have to select from the ingredients you have. So, whilst you can use the following as a guide, you can also make your own choices.

I have laid out these correspondences by colour and scent and then by birthsign so that you can cross-reference them according to your needs. Where you find several correspondences which match your needs, select the one(s) which are most meaningful to you. Trust your instincts as to what is appropriate.

Colours

★ **Pink:** Romantic love, emotional healing, friends, self-respect, fertility, inner peace

★ **Red:** The Goddess as Mother, fire, passion, lust, the south, fruitfulness, fertility, assertiveness, battle

★ **Orange:** The Sun, power, honour, money, work

★ **Gold:** The God, money, power, glory

★ **Yellow:** The Goddess as Maiden, Air, thought, the east, study, intellect, beginnings

★ **Green:** The God, earth, the body, growth, plants, the land, the north, money, fertility

★ **Turquoise:** The Goddess as Mother, fortune

★ **Blue:** The Goddess as Mother, water, emotion, the west, things of the sea

★ **Indigo:** Spiritual healing, study, learning, career

★ **Purple:** The Goddess as Crone, travel, exams

★ **Violet:** All healing, especially physical, rest, sleep, psychic ability

★ **White:** The Goddess as Maiden, peace

Silver: The Goddess, the Moon, female fertility, illusion, divination, protection

★ **Grey:** Air, weather, animals, birds

★ **Black:** The Goddess as Crone, the God as Lord of the Hunt, banishing, driving things away, closure

★ **Brown:** Earth, life, animals and animal healing

Many shades and colour variations have not been included here, but as I said earlier, it is important to make your own connections and build up your own correspondences.

Scents

There are even more potential scents than there are colours, so I have restricted myself to those which are either easy to buy in essential oil form or can be used in herb form or can be prepared at home.

★ **Basil:** Protection, study, concentration, memory, examinations, strength

★ **Bergamot:** To relieve depression, negativity, regret

★ **Black pepper:** Opening, stimulating, penetrating

★ **Camomile:** Rest, peace, soothing

★ **Cardamom:** Clarity, passion

★ **Cedar:** Stress relief, focus

★ **Cinnamon:** The Sun, psychic awareness

★ **Clary sage:** Balance, psychic ability

★ **Clove:** The Goddess as Crone, divination, prosperity

★ **Eucalyptus:** Colds and 'flu

★ **Fennel:** Travel, dietary control

★ **Frankincense:** The God, the Sun, purifying, protection, preparation for ritual, emotional healing, courage, insecurity

★ **Ginger:** Self-acceptance, courage, strength

★ **Jasmine:** The Goddess, the Moon, divination, dreams, love, self-acceptance

★ **Lavender:** Healing of all kinds, rest and sleep, travel

★ **Melissa:** The Goddess as Mother, woman, the female aspect

★ **Myrrh:** The Goddess as Crone, wisdom, knowledge, banishing negativity

★ **Neroli** (which is orange blossom and not to be confused with niaouli): Stress relief, romance, exhaustion

★ **Patchouli:** Clarity, passion

★ **Peppermint:** Strength, studying, mental stimulation

★ **Pine:** Mental cleansing

★ **Rose:** The Goddess as Mother, psychic awareness, romance, emotional healing, grief

★ **Rosemary:** Clarity, study, memory, indecisiveness

★ **Sage:** Prosperity, tonic, stimulating

★ **Sandalwood:** The God, the Moon, courage, self-confidence, perseverance

★ **Tea tree:** Antiseptic, healing infections

★ **Thyme:** Psychic awareness, travel, relief of colds and 'flu
★ **Ylang ylang:** The Goddess as Maiden, romance, self-appreciation, mental stability

Birthsigns

The colour combinations and scents for use when making birthsign candles are often given as listed below, but again you should work towards finding the ones which suit you and those people you are working for as individuals. Bear in mind that people born near the cusp of a sign (that is at the beginning or end of the dates shown) may actually belong to the preceding or following sign. In order to be certain you will need to calculate their sunsign from their date, time and place of birth, using an ephemeris, or you will need to get an astrologer to work it out for you. However, the following still provides a useful guideline for the majority of people.

★ **Aries:** 21 March–20 April; red, scarlet; cedar, frankincense, musk
★ **Taurus:** 21 April–21 May; green, orange; patchouli, rose, violet
★ **Gemini:** 22 May–21 June; yellow, orange; almond, lavender, sandalwood
★ **Cancer:** 22 June–22 July; amber, blue; jasmine, rose, sandalwood
★ **Leo:** 23 July–22 August; gold, orange; frankincense, musk, sandalwood
★ **Virgo:** 23 August–22 September; yellow, green; fennel, lavender, patchouli
★ **Libra:** 23 September–23 October; green, pink; rose, thyme, violet
★ **Scorpio:** 24 October–23 November; blue-green, red; clove, pine, rosemary
★ **Sagittarius:** 24 November–21 December; blue, violet; clove, cedarwood, nutmeg
★ **Capricorn:** 22 December–20 January; indigo, blue, violet; cypress, frankincense, lavender
★ **Aquarius:** 21 January–19 February; violet, rainbow; fennel, frankincense, pine
★ **Pisces:** 20 February–20 March; crimson, white; eucalyptus, jasmine, nutmeg

This is by no means a complete list of correspondences – there are many, many more, including days, weeks, animals, plants, and so on. For those of you who would like more information on correspondences, there are many books available which give listings, some of which are listed at the end of this book. I also recommend keeping a list of your own, so that you can see which work best for you.

Incense-Making

Incense is burned to create the atmosphere for working or ritual, to invoke the correct energies for the work you want to undertake and to attract the attention of the deity or deities you wish to work with. Generally speaking, then, incense is pleasing to the Gods. This does not always mean it is immediately pleasing to our senses, as we are trained to find certain smells pleasant and others unpleasant. For example, a two-year-old does not find the smell of excreta unpleasant unless trained to do so by their parents. So you may find that some incenses are not immediately 'nice' to smell, but if you can set aside your prejudices and focus on the work in hand you will find that an incense which suits your working is rarely unpleasant when burned in context because you know that it will enhance your work.

In addition to the Magical side of incense, there are many people who burn it just because they like the smell. Let's face it, perfumed air is bound to be more pleasant than the smell of old cooking or damp dog!

I am going to restrict myself to loose incense here, the kind that needs to be burnt on charcoal. Whilst it is possible to make your own joss sticks, incense papers or cones, and so on, it is extremely time-consuming and very messy. Besides, if you want to use incense sticks they are easy to come by and if you buy a good-quality brand you should get good-quality incense. It's easy to tell the difference – poor quality, or old, incense creates more smoke than scent and leaves an acrid taste in the mouth. Loose incense is comparatively easy to make, usually from a combination of flowers, leaves, roots, barks, woods and gums or resins. Occasionally oils and other ingredients such as honey are added, but sparingly, as you need a dry compound to burn, not a paste.

Because these are all natural ingredients, loose incense needs something to burn with and the most common is the 'self-igniting' charcoal block generally available from New Age stores. Do not use barbecue charcoal unless you are working outdoors, as it is far too smoky.

As charcoal creates a lot of heat when burned, you will also need a thurible, or container to burn your incense in. You can buy purpose-made ones or you can fill a small dish with sand and use this as a base to stop the heat ruining or even setting fire to your work surface.

The basic equipment needed to make loose incense is a pestle and mortar. This is so that you can grind the ingredients to an even size whilst mixing them. It is possible to improvise with a bowl and the 'heel' of a rolling pin, but you really shouldn't use an electric grinder as this reduces everything to a dust, not to mention leaves a taint on the equipment. You will also need some kind of sterile container to keep your finished incense in.

Unless you are making incense for a number of people, resist the temptation to make large quantities; whilst it doesn't go off quickly, its power will diminish over time and few of us use the stuff by the bucketful!

Most of the ingredients for loose incense can be bought from good herbalists and chemists, some, however, are harder to find and are more likely to be obtained mail order. Some herbs and flowers can be grown and dried yourself, but do make sure that they are fully dried, otherwise you risk your incense deteriorating rapidly or burning with huge clouds of smoke!

As with any aspect of Magical cooking, there is an element of trial and error with making your own incense. When blending ingredients use your sense of smell to see if the result seems harmonious with your intent, and before sealing the stuff away, burn a little to see whether it really does fit your needs.

There are whole books devoted to recipes for incense-making but here I am going to focus on some of the more commonly needed ones and on those for use at each of the Sabbats. Where possible I have tried to stick to ingredients which are not too difficult to find, or have indicated alternatives. Measurements are in 'parts' for dried ingredients, so that you can decide whether you want to use teaspoons or tablespoons, depending on the amount of incense you wish to create.

It is helpful if you can visualize your Magical goals when creating the incense and of course remember to label your finished product clearly. It is also useful to keep a record of your workings, not only in terms of the recipe you actually use, but also of the results you get, in this way you can build up a picture of what works for you.

Note that I have used the term 'burn incense' throughout – this does not mean that the incense should go up in flames, rather that it should smoulder gently, giving off gentle wafts of scented smoke, not huge clouds.

Banishment of Unwanted Influences

These can be external influences or simply the day-to-day emotional baggage that we all carry around with us.

3 parts frankincense
2 parts sandalwood
1 part bay
(bay leaves often need to be torn or cut up before adding to your pestle)
pinch of salt
(this may cause your incense to sparkle on the charcoal)

Preparation for Ritual

Use this to set the scene for Magical working, to create and/or enhance the mood.

3 parts frankincense
2 parts myrrh
1 part sandalwood
1 part rose petals
1/2 part cinnamon
1/2 part rosemary
1/4 part bay

Esbat Incense

For use at all Full Moon rituals. Ensure that the incense is burning before the Sacred Space is created.

2 parts frankincense
2 parts sandalwood
1 part rose petals
a few drops of musk oil

New Moon Incense

Burn this for New Moon workings or to honour the Goddess as Maiden.

2 parts frankincense
1 part sandalwood
1 part jasmine petals
1 part rose petals

Healing Incense

For use during Rites of Healing or when there is a need for physical, mental or emotional healing. However, do not burn incense in the room of someone in need of healing for a respiratory problem, as the residual fumes from the charcoal may irritate. Instead, perform the Magic in another location.

3 parts myrrh
1 part rose petals
1 part eucalyptus
a few drops of pine oil
a few drops of cedar oil

Power Incense

Use this to enhance any Magical working.

2 parts sandalwood
2 parts frankincense
1 part nutmeg
¼ part allspice
¼ part ginger (*use root ginger (wild ginger) if you can*)

Goddess Incense

There are as many Goddess incenses as there are female forms of the Divine. This is an all-purpose incense to invoke the Great Mother.

3 parts myrrh
3 parts sandalwood
2 parts cypress
1 part mint
a few drops of jasmine oil

God Incense

Similarly, there are many forms of incense for the God. Again, this is a general one to invoke the Lord of the Forest.

2 parts benzoin (*or gum arabic*)
1 part cedar
1 part pine
1 part juniper berries
2 drops patchouli oil

Incense for Divination

During any act of scrying, light the incense and then waft the smoke over your Tarot cards, runes or whatever tools of divination you are using. If you find the smoke from the incense irritates your eyes, place a lighted candle next to your thurible and the heat will encourage the smoke to rise.

2 parts sandalwood
1 part orange peel (*make sure you dry this thoroughly if making your own*)
1 part mace (*buy as the dried spice*)
1 part cinnamon
1 or 2 drops of clove oil

Hearth Incense

Burn this one for security and happiness in the home. It can also be used generally and makes a good present to give to others.

2 parts myrrh
1 part frankincense
1 part red sandalwood
1 part juniper berries
¹/₂ part orange flowers
¹/₂ part rose petals
¹/₂ part vanilla (*or a few drops of vanilla essence or extract*)

General Purpose Incense

Not everyone wants a large collection of different incense, in which case the following is a good choice for all workings.

3 parts frankincense
2 parts myrrh
1 part jasmine or rose petals
1 part cinnamon
a pinch of salt

Samhain, 31 October

2 parts frankincense
2 parts sandalwood
2 parts poppy seed
1 part gum arabic
1 part myrrh
$1/2$ part bay
$1/2$ part thyme
$1/4$ part jasmine flowers
$1/4$ part rose petals

Yule, 21 December

2 parts frankincense
2 parts pine needles
1 part cedar
1 part juniper berries
$1/4$ part cinnamon
$1/4$ part nutmeg
$1/4$ part ginger
$1/4$ part orange peel

Imbolg, 2 February

3 parts frankincense
1 part myrrh
1 part cinnamon
¹/₂ part sandalwood
¹/₂ part jasmine flowers
3 drops of sweet white wine or sherry

Oestara, 21 March

2 parts frankincense
1 part gum arabic
1 part sandalwood
¹/₂ part nutmeg
¹/₂ part orange oil
¹/₂ part rose petals

Beltane, 1 May

3 parts frankincense
2 parts sandalwood
1 part rose petals
1 part vanilla (*or a few drops of vanilla extract or essence*)
a few drops of jasmine oil
a few drops of neroli oil

Litha, 21 June

2 parts sandalwood
1 part wormwood

1 part camomile
1 part rose petals
a few drops of jasmine oil
a few drops of lavender oil

Lammas, 1 August

2 parts frankincense
1 part hops (*or sandalwood with a few drops of beer*)
1 part apple blossom
1 part blackberry leaves

Madron, 21 September

2 parts frankincense
1 part sandalwood
1 part cypress
1 part juniper
1 part pine
2 or 3 oak leaves

Ideally, incense should be stored in clean glass bottles and in a cool dark place. Add the date of making to the label, as well as the nature of the incense. In your record book make notes of the time you made each incense, the ingredients used and where you obtained them, the quantities used, the date and the phase of the Moon. Also note down how you felt at the time, as well as your impressions of the scent of the incense before and during burning. As some incenses age better than others, it is also an idea to make notes at the time of subsequent use, so that you can continue to develop your skills. Whilst it is always a good idea to experiment with new formulas, make sure that you burn a new blend in a well-ventilated place, close to a door or window. Then if you do create something which you deeply dislike, or which gives off a lot of smoke, you can prevent it from invading your whole house.

Feasting around the Wheel of the Year

'Ye shall dance, sing, feast… all in my name…'

Witches celebrate eight seasonal festivals called the Sabbats. Almost certainly the dates of these festivals, as celebrated today, are not the same as the ones that would have been celebrated before the arrival of the structured calendar and the universal system of counting the passage of time. The Major Sabbats of Samhain, Imbolg, Beltane and Lammas would have been timed by observing what actually happened in the world around. Hence Imbolg would have been celebrated when the first lambs were born, Beltane when the May came into bloom, Lammas when the first harvest was ready and Samhain when it was obvious that no more could be gathered before the winter storms. The Lesser Sabbats of Yule, Oestara, Litha and Madron all relate to the passage of the Sun, being the Winter and Summer Solstices and the Spring and Autumn Equinoxes. It is likely that these would have been celebrated two or three days after the actual event, when it was possible for people to have observed the changing length of day and night.

For those working in a group or Coven each of the Sabbats will be marked by a ritual followed by a feast. However, there are many Witches who like to share their seasonal feasting with friends or family as well as their group, not as an opportunity to preach or convert, but simply as a way of sharing the seasonal feeling. When planning such a celebration, bear in mind the theme of the festival and the colours associated with it as well as the foods of the season. You will also want to consider the type of occasion you are planning, be it informal party, family picnic or adults-only formal dinner.

In this chapter I will look at some of the foods and drinks which can be appropriate for these festivals, but you might also like to make adjustments to the 'menus' to reflect your own tastes and the seasonal fare typical of your region at that time. I have not given recipes for everything, as most of these dishes can be found in general cookery books or even purchased ready-made. These days, when we all have busy lives, it is just as relevant to buy festive foods as it is to labour long and hard in the kitchen to produce them yourself.

Try to achieve a variety of foods and a balance between savoury and sweet. Contrary to the fond hopes of some Witches of my acquaintance, Oestara is not a festival devoted entirely to the Great God Chocolate! Also, don't be afraid to share the burdens of shopping and paying for, preparing and cooking your feast. Some of the best parties happen when everyone mucks in and helps out.

Some of the recipes for drink will need to be started well in advance, unless you are planning to buy commercial ones. In some cases I have included quick recipes for these, as I know it is not always possible to brew from first principles.

Whilst I have looked to the origins of these festivals I have not restricted the menus to the foods that would have been available to our forebears. After all, if they had had the choice they wouldn't have stuck to the restricted diets imposed on them by circumstance. Our Craft traditions should not be only those with a long history but also those that have been incorporated over the years. The same applies to the other traditions associated with the festivals, the activities and games that can be used to take the celebration beyond just eating and drinking.

Why Follow a Seasonal Cycle?

In this day and age we put a great strain on nature and lay ourselves open to all kinds of other problems by having our food travel halfway round the world. Using local sources and seasonal foods means that we do not contribute to pollution by refrigerated vehicles, we lessen the risk of spreading of disease from one area to another and we do not make live animals suffer by cramming them into tiny spaces to travel hundreds of miles without water or a respite from what must be a terrifying experience. As I am writing this, northern Europe is in the grip of an outbreak of foot-and-mouth disease, an unpleasant contagion which has caused the premature slaughter of many healthy animals. But more distressing, to my mind at least, is the prospect that many animals will die of starvation or exposure because they, or their feed, cannot be moved. This is not because foot and mouth can infect people or because it kills the animals it infects, but in part because if we were to vaccinate against the disease we would be unable to export our meat to other countries. Given that Britain imports about as much lamb as it exports, this is obviously a problem exacerbated by the desire to eat out-of-season food.

If you wish to look at the issue from more personal basis, buying local foods which are in season means fewer transportation and storage costs. You have a better chance of knowing where the produce comes from and under what circumstances it was produced. You can also be said to be doing your local community a service, as you are directly supporting the people around you.

Additionally, one of the great advantages of using seasonally available foods is that your palate need not become jaded by a constant repetition of the same food season in, season out. I am not saying that you can't or shouldn't eat some things year round, rather that you will benefit from seasonally adjusting your diet to make the most of what is plentiful.

Of course some readers will live in areas that have a different seasonality and will have a different feel to the Wheel of the Year, but I hope that this will at least give some ideas as to how to approach the festivals.

The Eight Festivals

☆ ☆ ☆

Samhain

31 October

In the agricultural cycle this was the time when people gave a long hard look at what they had to last them through the cold days of winter. They would slaughter and salt down any animals that they felt either wouldn't make it through the winter or which they couldn't afford to support on the stocks from the harvest. So Samhain was a major feast and often the last time some fresh foods, especially meat, would be eaten until new life started again in spring.

The themes of this festival are: the end of the old year and start of the new; a time when the veil between the worlds of the living and the dead is at its thinnest and spirits can roam; a time of remembering those who have gone before by setting a place for them at our feast; a time of looking forward and of scrying (trying to see what will come).

At this time the Goddess takes on her robes of Crone and the God becomes the Hunter who will lead the Wild Hunt throughout the winter.

As Samhain has become more commercial through its modern counterpart of Halloween we find newer ideas which also give us themes for the festival: Jack o'Lanterns carved from pumpkins and food prepared to mimic all things ghoulish, ghostly or just plain scary. The old colours of this festival are dark red, purple and black for the Crone and dark green and black for the Hunter, to which have more recently been added the orange of autumn and of the pumpkin.

To Eat

Seasonal foods at this time include many kinds of game – pheasant, partridge, pigeon, hare, and so on – also seafood such as oysters and scallops. Whilst these things were wild and therefore inexpensive for most of our ancestors, today they are somewhat expensive. However, seasonal vegetables include the cheap and widely available Brussels sprouts, cabbage, parsnips, peas and winter potatoes. Also, the last of the autumn harvest should be available, apples and pears in particular. Some feasting suggestions for this season are:

★ Potatoes cooked in their jackets, either plain or stuffed. I like to scoop the insides out of the cooled potato, mash them and add beaten egg, lightly cooked vegetables, cheese, herbs and spices to make a variety of combinations.

★ Sausages. These would have been traditional and as they were intended as a way of preserving meat through the winter would have been full of herbs and spices. Find a good-quality butcher's where they make their own sausages and get a selection of the more interesting ones. Vegetarian sausages can also be found in many supermarkets and health stores.

★ Spare ribs, or pork belly strips grilled until really quite dark and served with traditional-style chutneys, those which include plums or are heavy on the onions.

★ Marrow stuffed with cheese(s), herbs, breadcrumbs and vegetables, served with spicy tomato sauce.

★ If you're having a Jack o'Lantern, use the insides to make pumpkin soup or a pumpkin pie heavily laced with cinnamon and nutmeg.

★ Baked apples stuffed with sweet mincemeat, wrapped in pastry and baked in the oven.

★ Fortune cookies – whilst not Wiccan in origin, these allow adults an uncomplicated look at what the future might bring.

Think of foods which can be dressed up to fit the Halloween theme:

★ Cut courgettes (zucchini) lengthways with zigzag cuts and paint with tomato purée, roast and you have crocodile mouths.

★ Make mini pizzas and decorate with olive eyes, anchovy hair and sweetcorn teeth to make ghastly faces.

★ Look out for black pasta (made with squid ink) and other commercially prepared items for the season.

To Drink

Strong red wine is suitable to honour the Goddess and the God at this season. You can even dress it up a bit by adding a small amount of brandy and some sugar.

Apples are very appropriate at several of the Sabbats and if you cut one across the core you will see a pentacle revealed in the middle. So try apple juice, cider or harvest moonshine (*see below*).

If this is a family event, make non-alcoholic 'cocktails' of fruit juice and fizzy drinks. Adding some bright food colouring will make these into devilish enough drinks to suit even the most ghoulish child (watch out for those allergic to food colourings, though!) My favourite is demon's blood: ginger beer with apple and orange juice coloured a spectacular dark green. Food colouring can also be added to milk drinks, so try milk blended with a banana and a scoop of ice cream, coloured vivid red, as the vampire's drink of blood.

Harvest Moonshine

This is a rich heady blend of fruit and honey and is served at many of the Sabbats. It is well worth following the traditional recipe, as it has a much better flavour than the quick method. You can either make it in bulk or start off several batches throughout the course of the year. The quick version is tasty but lacks the well-rounded flavour of the original and is quite expensive.

Harvest Moonshine: Traditional Method

3 large oranges
2 lemons
3 large apples
3 cinnamon sticks
3 cardamoms
12 cloves
3 nutmegs
8 pints (20 cups) water
4–6 lb honey
1 oz fresh or wine yeast blended in ¼ pint tepid water

Take the rind, flesh and juice of the oranges and lemons, coarsely chop and discard the white pith. Chop the apples. Add, together with the cinnamon sticks, cardamoms, cloves and nutmegs, to 4 pints (10 cups) of water, bring to the boil and simmer for 30 minutes. Strain •• and add a further 4 pints of cold water. Then stir in the honey. Next add the yeast solution.

When it is thoroughly dissolved, place the fluid in a sterilized demi-john with a fermentation lock. Demi-johns can usually be found in second-hand shops and after thorough washing can be sterilized using the tablets sold to sterilize baby feeding bottles. If you haven't a fermentation lock, you can improvise by tying a plastic bag over the neck in such a way as to leave room for gas to expand but no air to enter.

Place in a warm dark place and leave for at least six months. After about six weeks you should see small bubbles rising to the surface; after about six months this activity should have ceased. If it has not stopped, wait a little longer.

When you are absolutely sure it has stopped fermenting, decant into sterile bottles with cork tops – the kind sold with port or sherry in are usually ideal. Leave a further week or so to be sure no further fermentation starts. You'll know if it does because the corks will lift, or even pop!

Harvest Moonshine: **Quick Method**

At the point marked •• in the traditional recipe, omit the extra water, add the honey, cool the liquid and add 2 bottles of vodka. Decant into the cork-topped bottles and leave for one month, just to check no fermentation has started.

To Make Merry

Samhain is definitely party time for old and young alike. There are celebrations, both religious and secular, around the world at this time; we celebrate Halloween, Guy Fawkes' night and All Hallows' Eve, but you will find similar celebrations almost everywhere, reflecting the continuity of this feast of the dead.

One very contentious subject at this time of year is trick or treating. I personally would never advocate indiscriminate trick or treating. It is not safe for youngsters to go around knocking on strangers' doors and asking for sweets – besides, it's exactly what you've been telling them not to do for the other 364 days of the year. Additionally, some people are intimidated by the idea, let alone the sight, of a group of youngsters demanding treats on their doorstep in the dark. Having said that, if you can get together with other parents and arrange that your combined, and supervised, horde only knocks on the doors of those who are expecting them, a good time can be had by all.

A more simple treat for children and the young at heart is bobbing for apples, either in water (cover the floor with plastic) or on strings suspended in the doorway. A variant on this is to place wrapped sweets on the surface of a shallow bowl of flour and watch the whitened faces emerge. Encourage the participants to keep their hands behind their backs, but never tie them there in case they need to free themselves in a hurry.

This is also a traditional time for scrying or divination of all kinds, so if no one in your group is going to be offended, perhaps someone can read the Tarot or you can use another form of looking into the future.

Teenagers can try seeing if they can find the initial of their future partner by peeling an apple in one go and throwing the peel over their shoulder to see what shape it lands in.

Fancy dress is an excellent way of breaking the ice. Even the most self-conscious seem to be relaxed about dressing up as a vampire for Halloween. Younger guests love having their faces painted and can also be encouraged to make masks (use paper plates as your starting-point) and other props.

For a really messy children's party, play Guess the Body Parts. In a poorly lit room, with plenty of plastic or paper on the floor, all the guests close their eyes and take it in turns to dip their fingers into intestines (cold spaghetti), eyeballs (lychees (litchis) or peeled grapes, teeth (dried corn or confectionery 'dentures'), and brains (jelly (jello)). Use your imagination and make sure there are plenty of damp cloths and towels around.

Most older children and adults love horror stories, so try getting everyone to bring their own short story to the session. It's quite often a good idea to do this in a gloomy room with a lighter area where anyone who becomes nervous can take refuge.

Yule

21 December

This is the Winter Solstice, the point at which the hours of daylight stop decreasing and start to lengthen. The actual date will vary from year to year, but many celebrate it on 21 December anyway. This is when we celebrate the rebirth of the Sun. It is the forerunner of Christmas. At this time the Lord of Holly, who presides over the darkening year, gives way to the Lord of Oak who presides over the lighter days.

Traditional colours for this festival are gold, dark and light green for the God and still dark red for the Goddess.

To Eat

Because we are in the midst of winter the traditional emphasis was on preserved foods laid down from the end of the harvest. Traditional European feasts would not have included turkey, but more likely boar, salt beef or game birds, with winter vegetables, dried pulses and nuts.

As Christmas comes hard on the heels of Yule it is a good idea to try not to emulate that festival's foods, but rather to provide something different. Honey-glazed roast pork and beef and ale pie are both very traditional. Roast goose is excellent if you have a large oven and a large gathering. Before cooking baste it with boiling water and then roast it on a rack over a roasting tin (broiler tray) to allow the fat to run off. Also, have foods with a sunny theme: bread baked in a the shape of the Sun, sunflower and other seeds roasted with spices, golden cheeses. Fruit preserved from the summer – whole plums in brandy syrup, pears in wine, greengages and gooseberries in honey syrup – can be served on its own, as an accompaniment to meat dishes or as the basis for fruit pies and puddings. Dried fruit, too, is useful – take a selection and soak overnight in cider, warm through and serve with chopped nuts, sour cream or yoghurt.

Plum Pudding

Here all the dried fruit would be combined with a little precious flour to make a feasting dessert. This would usually have been made quite early in the year, both to use up the remaining stock from the winter before, rather than eating into this year's preserves, and to allow the pudding maximum time to mature. In our family we often concluded one year's festivities by making the pudding(s) for the next, some of which would be kept for our own use, some of which would make presents to be given prior to Yule.

To make a really rich alternative, start by soaking pricked prunes (which are only dried plums) in warm tea overnight. Take them out and strain them, then bottle them in brandy with a little sugar. Leave this for three to six months. Next take any modern Christmas pudding recipe and replace all the dried fruit ingredients with your soaked prunes and all the liquid ingredients with the brandy the prunes were stored in. Keep the dry ingredients as per the recipe. Make and pre-cook the pudding as usual and store until needed.

If you want an even more traditional feel, make a spherical pudding. Before cooking, line your pudding basin (ovenproof bowl) with greaseproof (waxed) paper and a clean tea towel, and pull the paper and cloth into a bunch at the top and tie securely with string, making a ball shape. Tie the securing string to a wooden spoon balanced over the top of the pudding basin (so that your pudding cannot relax) and cook it that way.

Yule Log

Another key component to this feast is the Yule log. Originally this would not have been a part of the eating side of the feast (*see* below in Activities) but a chocolate-covered Swiss roll (jelly roll) has become part of our modern feast.

To Drink

Mulled ale or wine is very traditional and helps to keep the winter's chill at bay, and when blended with a little brandy forms the Wassail Cup. Mulled cider is also very tasty. Take a couple of pints of cider, add cloves, cinnamon (try to get the sticks as the ready ground variety tends to lie on the top or form a sediment), and nutmeg, and warm through slowly and gently. Whatever kind of Wassail Cup you are making, remember never to let it come to the boil, as that removes all the alcohol!

Less traditional, but still very nice, is hot chocolate with a big pinch of ground cinnamon or a teaspoon of your favourite liqueur.

For ritual purposes, mead or harvest moonshine (*see above*) make a drink to welcome the return of the Sun.

To Make Merry

Decorate the house with evergreens, especially holly, with its red berries, which celebrates both Goddess and God. Also mistletoe, which has long been considered sacred as it grows between earth and sky. Buy this rather than collect it yourself to preserve the wild plants.

Rising before dawn to greet the Sun is one way of celebrating this festival, but is not for the faint-hearted in midwinter. Some groups like to drum up the Sun, but it is important that this is not done where you are going to disturb those who need their sleep! We often follow this with a very non-traditional 'feast' of fried egg-and-bacon sandwiches washed down with hot chocolate laced with brandy. Not exactly health food, but definitely a warming reward for rising early enough to climb somewhere to see the Sun's first appearance over the horizon.

The lighting of the Yule log often forms a part of the Yule Ritual, or can be incorporated into a family event. You need a piece of sturdy wood, part of a cut branch, with the base levelled to make it stable. Securely fix a candle for each participant on top. Each person lights their candle and makes a wish for the coming season.

Plays and Mumming used to be a key part of this season. Dark is giving way to light at this time and the battle of the Oak and Holly Kings (with Oak winning), the tale of Gawain and the Green Knight, and the battle of St George and the Dark Knight can all be re-enacted. All three of these have the same basic theme: the lords overseeing the darkening days and the lightening days battle, with the latter winning. But as the two are immortal brothers, the victory is temporary and the battle replayed at the Summer Solstice, with the other being the victor at that time.

It used to be traditional to appoint a Lord of Misrule to oversee the Yule festivities. This would be a person selected at random whose role was to ensure that much fun and laughter took place at the festival. They could set tasks, play pranks and jokes, or demand that each member of the assembly took turns to provide the amusement for all. Alternatively, a King and Queen for the day might be appointed, whose roles were much the same. Originally they would be 'chosen' by the finding of a dried bean and pea located within a cake made especially for the purpose. This is the origin of the silver tokens often added to the more modern Christmas pudding.

Imbolg

2 February

Now we see the first signs of life returning to the land, the first buds on the trees, the first flowers peeking through the frozen earth. The sheep are in lamb and in some areas the first lambs have already been born, so we know that spring will come again. At this time the Goddess changes from Crone to Maiden, full of hope and promise of life to come, and we celebrate her return with candles, hence the more modern Candlemas.

Imbolg is also the feast of the Irish Fire Goddess Bride (pronounced *Bre-ed*), known as Brigantia to the Celtic Britons and Bridget when she was Christianized.

The colours of the season are white and yellow for the Goddess and light green for the God, who is once more young and carefree.

To Eat

Our forebears would have been rejoicing, for although fresh food would not have been plentiful at this festival, at least some would have been available to enliven the preserved diet of the winter months.

Lamb is ideal for this feast. Cook it simply, adding sprigs of fresh rosemary during the cooking, or serve with rosemary or lavender jelly. Also look for young fresh vegetables to steam or cook in foil parcels.

Choose foods which are light in colour and texture – omelettes, quiche, pancakes, etc. Pancakes, like many foods with three key ingredients, are very appropriate for celebrating the Goddess in her three aspects. They do not have to be sweet; they can also be savoury. For a savoury pancake, make the base slightly thicker than usual, place it on an ovenproof plate and top it with thinly sliced onions, peppers, sweetcorn and grated cheese. Place it under a hot grill until the cheese melts. Remember, whereas Yule had golden yellow and dark green, Imbolg should have pale creamy yellow and light green.

'Champagne Jelly'

This really captures the feeling of the season. You can make your jelly from gelatine and sparkling fruit juice (apple or white grape). To determine the amount of juice, follow the instructions on the gelatine packet, but only warm a third of the juice, adding the rest cold to preserve the bubbles. Place a couple of pieces of fruit – sliced apple, grape or pear – into a wine glass, half fill with the still-warm jelly and then place the wine glasses carefully in the fridge so that they are at a slant. When the jelly has set, which should be at an angle when the glasses are stood upright once more, fill the remaining space with whipped plain yoghurt or crème fraîche. Just before serving, top with a single piece of the fruit.

Frozen Fruit Bombe

This is another excellent dessert which emulates the return of life from the frozen ground. Take dried fruits which have been marinated overnight in sweet white wine or pale cream sherry, drain well and add to slightly melted good-quality vanilla ice cream. Blend in well (work quickly before the ice cream turns to soup!), pack into a pudding basin, then return to the freezer for several hours or overnight. Allow to stand in a cool room for about an hour before serving. If you can, decorate with the petals of one or two fresh flowers, but do check they are not poisonous first.

Candle Cake

In some Craft traditions the High Priestess will arrive in Circle at this time swathed in black (representing the Crone) and during the ritual her maidens will unveil her, revealing robes of white, and crown her with a circle of lights, literally a crown of candles (representing the Maiden). This somewhat risky procedure can be symbolized by preparing a circular cake which has small white candles all around the top (one or more for each person present) and arrives at the table covered with a dark cloth. The cloth is removed and the candles lit, each one being a wish for the coming season. The cake itself should also be light in colour, and if iced, should be decorated with symbols of the season.

To Drink

Again, the drinks should represent the freshness of the season and should be full of life and enthusiasm. Champagne, if you can afford it, is ideal, otherwise sparkling white wine, lemonade or mineral water are suitable. In fact the latter is very appropriate, as this is the time when the spring thaw commences and ice-cold bubbling water would have been one of the signs in some regions. As mineral water is not most people's idea of a celebratory drink, though, try adding a squeeze of fresh citrus juice – lemon, orange, lime or grapefruit – or even some white grape or apple juice.

As the weather is still not warm in early February, fruit teas are also good at this season and can be chosen for their properties (*see* Chapter 9, 'Brews and Teas'), or simply for their taste.

To Make Merry

At Yule the spark of light was reborn, at Imbolg we celebrate it coming to strength. Having said that, this is still not a warm time of year for most, so whilst we may enjoy a short walk through the snow or slush to see the signs of burgeoning life, the emphasis is on activities which take place largely indoors!

The above-mentioned crown of lights is not really practical for most people – just the thought of moving around with a number of burning candles on your head should be enough to make anyone nervous! However, it can easily be replaced by a chaplet (or circlet) of flowers. These can be woven together on their own or can be threaded onto a pre-bought wicker circle. You'll find these in most good florists. Again, choose whites, yellows and pale greens for your theme. If, like me, you feel this is a lot of trouble to go to for just a few hours of flower-life, you can always use silk flowers or even go the whole way and make your own paper ones.

Children can make their own candle crown by taking a length of cardboard to go around the head and two cross pieces which go over the crown,and then securing an empty toilet-roll holder (as the candle) in the centre with tape. This should all be painted white and the crown part can be decorated with yellow and silver flowers, lambs, etc. Into the top of the 'candle' fix a 'flame' of orange paper.

In many parts of Europe well dressing still takes place. This ritual is the remnant of pre-Christian celebrations of Bride. Unfortunately this rarely happens around Imbolg, but do check to see if there is something happening in your area. As an alternative, you can always make an excursion to a nearby well to cast a coin or two into the waters. The ancient tradition is believed to appease the spirits of the water and to grant wishes for the coming season, so long as the wishes are not spoken aloud.

Oestara

21 March

This is the festival of the Saxon Dawn Goddess Eostar (also known as Eostra or Ostara). Her symbols are the egg and the hare, which was later softened to the rabbit in modern festivals. Eostar is a Goddess of Fertility and this is a festival not just of fertility of the body and the land, but also of the mind, of hopes and wishes. This was traditionally a time when the first seeds would be sown.

It is also the Spring (or Vernal) Equinox, when day and night, light and dark, are equal, and it is this balance that we seek in our lives. It is the time when we turn out the old (the origins of spring cleaning) and take on the new. In the Craft we do this in terms of casting off old fears and worries, outworn guilt and completed projects, and taking on new hopes and aspirations. Just as the land is celebrating a rebirth, so do we in our personal lives.

As this is one of the equinoxes and therefore an astronomical event, the actual date of Oestara may vary from year to year. It is almost certain that our forebears would have had to wait until a couple of days afterwards in order to be certain that the length of day had indeed exceeded the length of night.

The colours of this festival are yellows and light greens.

To Eat

Again, lamb is very appropriate, as is humanely raised veal, and both should be served with plenty of spring vegetables. It used to be traditional, especially in Leicestershire, to eat hare pie for this festival, but I would counsel against this as, not only are hares especially sacred to the Goddess at this time, but also there are few enough of them around as it is.

At this time of year dandelions and nettles are springing up. Rather than simply uprooting them, put them to use in the kitchen. Cook nettle tops in the same way as spinach – a pan full of leaves with a tablespoon of water will cook down into a couple of portions to be served with butter and a sprinkling of lemon juice and pepper.

Young dandelion leaves are also excellent in salad. Make sure you only use this season's growth as the old ones can be tough and bitter. Dandelion leaves make an excellent tea as well.

Nettle Soup

1 lb nettle leaves
2 cloves of finely chopped garlic
1 oz butter
¼ pint vegetable stock (*broth*)
1 pint whole milk

Wash and chop the nettle leaves and fry with the garlic in the butter. Add the stock, bring to the boil and simmer for 5 minutes. Blend or push through a sieve. Add the milk and heat gently. Do not allow to boil. Serve with a swirl of cream and some very fresh bread.

Simnel Cake

Simnel cake is also cooked at this time of year. This is just a basic sponge-cake mix with nutmeg, cinnamon, ginger and mixed spice. Two cakes are baked, sandwiched together with marzipan and decorated with marzipan eggs.

Marzipan

It really is better if you can take the time to make your own marzipan, which tastes of almonds, rather than using the manufactured version, which tastes of chemicals.

½ **lb icing (*confectioner's*) sugar**
½ **lb caster (*granulated*) sugar**
1 lb ground almonds
1 tsp vanilla essence or extract
2 eggs
lemon juice

Sift the icing sugar into a bowl and add the caster sugar and ground almonds. Add the vanilla essence. Lightly beat the eggs and add, together with enough lemon juice to make a stiff dough. Knead lightly and roll out. Try not to let the paste dry out, as it will crack.

As I mentioned earlier, contrary to the opinion/hope of many Witches it is possible to eat things other than chocolate to celebrate Oestre. Having said that, falling as it does so close to the time of year when the shops are full of chocolate eggs and rabbits, it would be unreasonable to avoid this type of 'food for the Gods'! So do incorporate chocolate into your feast.

To Drink

To honour the Goddess and the God at this time you should be looking for a young fruity red wine. Fruit wines and beers (not 'alco-pops') of all kinds are also seasonal. If you had the time, and inclination, to make some at harvest time, they should now be at their best.

Keen wine or beer makers could start preparing dandelion or nettle wine, or even nettle beer, for later drinking.

To Make Merry

If you have willing friends and family, this is an excellent time to hold a gardening party. This is an activity where everyone has a role to play, from the eldest, who can dispense wisdom (and much-needed refreshment), to the youngest, who always enjoy playing in the soil and planting seeds. The soil can be cleared of dead plants and leaves left over from winter, overgrowth can be trimmed back and young plants and seeds started off. As this is intended as a working celebration, get everyone to bring along something for a group meal at the end of your labours.

If you feel this is too much to ask of those around you, then perhaps you can make up small packets of seeds to give to your friends and family in honour of the season.

A game greatly loved by the young is the egg hunt. This can take place either indoors or out. Make sure that you have plenty of small eggs, some well hidden and some easy to find for the very small. You might also want to 'handicap' older children by making them wait to start hunting a bit later than the tinies.

Egg decorating is another traditional activity for children. Make sure you have plenty of very hard-boiled (hard-cooked) eggs, paints and brushes and give a prize for the best decorated egg. These eggs can then be used in the egg hunt, so that you don't have to risk some children finding, and eating, so many chocolate eggs that they make themselves unwell. Instead chocolate eggs can be given out as prizes and/or one can be given to each child who participates.

Another egg game that people of all ages can join in is the old-fashioned egg and spoon race. This can be played using hard-boiled or chocolate eggs. A really humorous alternative is to get your guests to push the eggs along the ground using their noses, or elbows.

Beltane

1 May

Beltane is the second most important festival of the year. The Goddess sheds her robes of Maiden and takes on those of Mother, the God casts aside the irresponsibility of youth and takes his place as her consort, and we celebrate their marriage. Beltane is a fertility festival and it used to be that all the unattached men and women would dress in green and spend the night in the woods seeking a partner. This was euphemistically called 'gathering in the May' and this is why it is considered unlucky to bring May blossom into the house on this day, as it indicated an unsuccessful preceding night! Children born as a result of May eve were considered to be especially blessed, as they were considered children of the God. This tradition then became celebrated in the choosing of a May Queen, who then selected her partner the May King, and the two presided over the May celebrations. These celebrations would also include dancing around the Maypole, another fertility ritual which is still being revived in Britain after Cromwell banned it in the seventeenth century.

In keeping with the marriage of the Goddess and the God, many modern Witches and Pagans will celebrate their wedding, or Handfasting as it is called, at this time.

Beltane is also the festival of the Solar God Bel, and it was traditional for bonfires to be lit and the cattle and livestock driven between them to ensure their fertility. The people would jump these fires for their own fertility.

Like Samhain, Beltane is also a time when the veil between the worlds is thin, only this time it is the spirits of jest and humour who may step through. Trickster Gods such as Pan, Puck and Loki can be invoked at this time, but beware of the consequences, as the Gods have a sense of humour too!

The colours of this festival are bright red and silver for the Goddess, and green and gold for the God, alternatively blue and gold for the Goddess and red and gold for the God.

To Eat

As this festival celebrates the marriage of the Goddess and the God it really is the time for a major feast, a wedding supper. If the weather is fine enough, this could be the first picnic of the year, which would also facilitate some of the traditional Beltane games, which are best played outside.

Roast pork is a good meat for this festival, served traditional style with all the trimmings and of course a good home-made apple sauce. Serve lightly cooked spring vegetables and herbs, or use them to make soups, pies and salads. Also try adding fresh herbs to ice cream or sorbet.

Cucumber Soup

1 small finely chopped onion
1 cucumber
1/2 oz butter
1/4 pint vegetable stock (broth) (*or water with a good pinch of salt*)
1/2 handful fresh chopped parsley
1 pint milk

Peel and finely chop the cucumber, finely chop the onion and fry in the butter until softened but not brown. Add the vegetable stock and parsley, bring to the boil, then simmer gently for 5 minutes. Push through a sieve or blend, then add the milk.

If serving hot, warm through but do not allow to boil. If serving chilled, add another good pinch of salt and place in the fridge for a couple of hours. Just before serving, add a large swirl of single (light) cream. Use celery as an alternative to cucumber.

Chicken recipes are good for this time of year too. Try roasting with an onion inside, or with garlic and rosemary slipped between the meat and skin of the breast. Paint the outside of the bird with a sweet chilli, plum or hoisin sauce. If you are planning a picnic, try chicken sandwiches with rowan or lavender jelly, a salad of lettuce, tansy and rocket (arugula) leaves, or sandwiches of sliced chicken, boiled egg and mayonnaise.

Elderflower heads can be dipped in beaten egg and flour, then deep fried and served with caster sugar and cream. Elderflowers can also be used to flavour ice cream or sorbet, or to make elderflower wine.

To Drink

Mead, often called the honeymoon drink, is most appropriate at this time. Otherwise look for sweet wines and liqueurs. Elderflower cordial made with a sparkling mineral water is excellent too.

To Make Merry

If numbers permit, elect a May Queen – this is often best done by drawing lots so that no envy is generated – and allow her to choose her May King. These two are crowned and then rule over the festivities. You can make this ceremony even more elaborate by preparing thrones and cloaks for the 'royal' couple.

Daisies, those small white flowers which are the bane of most proud lawnkeepers, are plentiful at this time. Organize a daisy chain competition with prizes for the longest, most attractive chains.

If you can, set up a Maypole. A simple version can often be produced using a garden umbrella stand with a long broom handle wired securely onto it. To the top tie a number of long ribbons or streamers and have half your number dancing clockwise whilst the other half dance anti-clockwise and weave in and out of the first group. Place a flower garland at the top of the pole. As the ribbons become twisted around the pole the garland should descend gracefully. Unless you have several experienced May dancers, this will almost certainly not go smoothly, but the general confusion and laughter usually serve to lighten the proceedings.

As May day is once more taking its place as a festival on the calendar, look out for regional events. It can be great fun to take a party of people to a pageant, parade or festival.

Litha

21 June

This is the Summer Solstice. From this point onwards the hours of daylight will decrease in length and the hours of darkness increase. This is the height of the Sun's power and in the northern hemisphere summer itself really begins at this time. At this point the battle of Oak and Holly is once more enacted, only this time Lord Oak gives way to Lord Holly.

The colours of this festival are golden yellows and oranges and gold itself for the God, while the Goddess wears red.

To Eat

Try to keep a golden theme to your feast: carrots, oranges, bread in the shape of the Sun. As summer is now really upon us, this is definitely the time to try for an outdoor picnic or barbecue. Provide a plentiful range of salads using as much imagination as you can: green-leaf salad with plenty of herbs tossed in a little orange juice, tomatoes sliced and dusted with freshly ground pepper and salt, cucumber with olives and goat's cheese with an olive oil dressing, also sliced apple and walnuts in yoghurt, grated carrot in orange and lemon juice, mixed lettuce with apple and melon, cooked and chilled chickpeas (garbanzo beans) with olive oil and garlic dressing, couscous with lemon juice, olives, rock salt and black pepper, potato and anchovy salad with a tomato dressing.

If you are holding a barbecue, you can avoid the common problem of food being black on the outside and red in the middle by marinating meat and pre-cooking it in a microwave, so that the barbecue has only to brown and heat it through. Add sprigs of fresh herbs to the coals to further enhance the flavour of the food.

Vegetables can be prepared, sprinkled with herbs and a little oil, then wrapped in tinfoil (aluminium foil) before being placed on the barbecue. Similarly, fish can be prepared, stuffed with herbs and spices and wrapped in tinfoil to cook. Children's favourites such as chicken nuggets or shapes can also be cooked in foil. You might like to try making your own beefburger mix. Chill it well and then roll it out and cut it into shapes for the youngsters.

Summer is also the time for ice cream. You can make your own from first principles or alternatively customize shop-bought ice cream by allowing it to soften a little and add your own ingredients before stirring well and refreezing. All kinds of sweet biscuits can be crushed and added – try chocolate chip cookies or malted milk biscuits. Summer fruit like strawberries and raspberries can be sieved or blended, but to add a citrus flavour it is better to use thin slivers of rind and a little juice. Alternatively, make fruit up into a syrup by taking equal amounts of sugar and water and warming through until fully dissolved. Add your fruit and cool before adding to the ice cream. Sweet herbs like mint or saffron and spices like cinnamon or nutmeg can also add a different flavour. If using dried ingredients like grated coconut, make sure you leave a little time for the flavour to blend in. You could also add chopped up pieces of your favourite chocolate bar. Buy the best-quality ice cream you can afford. Vanilla works well with almost any added ingredients, but you can always 'dress up' other flavours too. Try adding crushed praline (hard toffee/crisp candy with nuts) and peaches to coffee ice cream, or sliced pineapple to lemon sorbet.

To Drink

In ritual the Goddess and the God will be honoured with strong red wine, sherry or port, but for celebrating and feasting golden liquids are appropriate – cider, light beer, white and rosé wines (especially sweet), pale sherry and mead, also fruit juices, especially if made from summer fruits. Look out for fruit squashes, preferably the kind which actually do contain some fruit juice, to mix with sparkling mineral water and, for adults only, vodka.

If the weather is warm, 'cut' strong wines, sherry, etc., with lemonade or mineral water. Add a few pieces of fresh fruit or mint leaves for that summer cocktail feel. For young people remember that not only does hot weather increase thirst, but so does over-strong squash (fruit drink).

Try a 'cucumber sandwich': one part dry gin, three to five parts tonic water and two or three slices of cucumber.

Lemonade

Home-made lemonade really does taste best. You will need:

3 lemons
6 oz sugar
1 ½ pints water

Gently wash the lemons and peel the rind thinly. Put the rind and the sugar into a heatproof jug (pitcher). Bring the water to the boil and pour over. Cover and cool, stirring occasionally. Then add the juice of the same three lemons. Strain and serve chilled.

To Make Merry

As at Yule it is traditional at Litha to rise at dawn to greet the Sun. However, unlike Yule, sunrise is very early, so this is perhaps a rite best left to the dedicated few who do not have work or other commitments which require them to have had a full night's sleep. However, if Litha falls on a convenient day, then perhaps the best way to celebrate is with an all-night party where the survivors can get to bed after greeting the dawn.

The battle of the Oak and Holly Kings can be re-enacted, as at Yule, and you can make this a contest where everyone can join in. Split your number into two teams and have them compete in either one game or in a selection (always make this an uneven number of games to avoid a tie). Make the competition as energetic as you like. Why not try physical activities like tug of war, or races and mental competitions like chess, draughts (checkers) or bridge. For the young you could have snakes and ladders or ludo. Don't make adult games too grown up – often more fun is generated by an egg and spoon race than a strenuous or serious game.

If you are outside, then set children off on a 'treasure hunt'. Give them a list of objects to gather which are likely to be found in the environment – a red stone, a round pebble, a feather, a forked twig, two daisies, a coin, and so on. Caution them not to cut wild flowers or break down living plants and then reward the child who comes back first with all the requirements. Alternatively, if the surroundings seem suitable, get them to work together to build a face of the Sun from pebbles, twigs, etc.

Lammas

1 August

This is the festival of the first of the harvest and as such would have been a time of great rejoicing. Whole communities, men, women and children together, would have gathered to harvest the crops and to celebrate afterwards. Lammas has also been called 'loaf-mass', which is a reminder of just how important the first grain and its bread were. Lammas is also the festival of Lugh the Sun God, and of the Sacrificial King who is still represented by the gingerbread man. The Lammas loaf might be shaped as a sheaf of wheat, the Sun or even a man to represent any of the Lammas themes.

The colours of this festival are golds, yellows and oranges for the God and red for the robes of the bountiful Mother which the Goddess wears.

To Eat

Central to this feast must be the loaf. However, a word of caution to those of you about to embark on making this for yourself: take as your starting-point the size of tin which fits into your oven. As you can probably guess, we had to bake our Lammas loaf in two parts and then try to put them together for the table! For bread recipes and other ideas *see* Chapter 7, 'Breads, Cakes and Biscuits to Honour the Goddess and the God'.

Rabbit is a traditional meat for this season, as rabbits were driven from the fields by the harvesters and no free source of food would have been wasted. This is a meat which is only just appearing in our shops again after a number of years of being unpopular. Rabbit has quite a strong flavour and unless very young can be a bit tough, so it is best stewed or braised. Soaking the meat in lightly salted water for a couple of hours will make it more palatable. Try cooking pieces of rabbit with potato and root vegetables in an ale sauce, or cook it very slowly with prunes and cherries, adding a dash of brandy just before serving. Rabbit can also be used in the following pasty recipe, together with leek and potato, parsley and other mixed herbs.

Also traditional at this time would have been meat pies and pasties – anything which could be taken into the fields for the feast. Whilst Cornish pasties do not derive from this festival, they are an excellent way of celebrating it. Unless you are lucky and have a really good local pasty-maker, don't use the shop-bought ones – they are so 'generic' as to be virtually tasteless compared with the real thing.

Cornish-Style Pasties

12 oz finely cut steak
4 oz peeled diced potato
1 finely chopped onion
pinch salt
black pepper
12 oz shortcrust pastry

Mix the steak, potato and onion well. Season really well with the salt and pepper, and blend together. Take the shortcrust pastry and divide into four. Roll out into rounds about 8 inches across. Divide your meat mixture between the four rounds and fold the pastry in half over them. Flute the edges together with your fingers to make a really strong seal, either at the side or the top. Bake in the oven at 220°C/425°F for 15 minutes to brown and then at 170°C/325°F for a further hour. If the pasties start to get too brown, cover them with tinfoil 'hats' until 15 minutes before the end of cooking.

There are many variations on this recipe and much debate as to what constitutes a 'real' Cornish pasty. However, as you're making this for yourself and your friends, you can add or substitute anything which takes your fancy. Carrot or swede (squash) can replace some of the potato, finely cut lamb can replace steak, and so on. You can also try less obvious ideas such as mutton and chestnut (add a few breadcrumbs to absorb the fattiness of the mutton). A really good vegetarian version can be made using potato, onion, carrot, broccoli, sweetcorn and some coarsely grated cheese, in which case reduce the total cooking time to 45 minutes. Alternatively, try Stilton, leek and pinenuts or mixed mushrooms with tomato and chilli.

It is said that the original pasty was a complete meal in itself, having a savoury end and a sweet end. As this is an idea that few people really fancy these days, you can get around it by also producing a sweet version of the pasty. Use a sweet shortcrust pastry and fill with the fruit and nuts of the season. Add a few breadcrumbs or crushed plain sweet biscuit to make sure that the insides are not too liquid.

This is also the time of year to make the most of the fruits which are in season, such as apples, blackberries, blackcurrants, cherries, damsons, elderberries, gooseberries, greengages, mulberries (if you can find them), pears, plums, raspberries and strawberries. Slice them into salads, cook them in pies and pastries. If you're feeling adventurous, serve stewed fruit with meat, not just apples with pork but also lightly cooked plums or damsons, pears or cherries with chicken. Try crab apple jelly with pork or chicken or rowan jelly with stronger meats such as beef (*see* Chapter 11, 'Herb Sachets and Gifts', for a recipe and variations for making savoury and sweet jellies).

To Drink

A good strong red wine is the drink with which to honour the Goddess and the God, but perhaps it is best held back for more formal ways of marking this feast.

Cider really is the traditional drink of this festival. With its golden colour and apple flavour a good cider is redolent with the smells and tastes of the first of the harvest. Most commercially-made cider is an acceptable drink, but if you want the true flavour of Lammas try to find a farm-made cider or scrumpy. Alternatively, mix a strong cider with apple juice to really bring out the 'apple-iness'.

Real ales are also appropriate. These days you can find many new varieties of ale which are stronger in both taste and smell than the 'canned' beer of recent times. Look out for fruit beers, too, as these are also closer to the traditional drink of our agricultural past.

To Make Merry

Use straw to make your own Corn King who can be slain to symbolize the sacrificial king of old. This can be done in ritual or as a game where the contestants throw a sickle at the image until one manages to remove his head, but do remember to take precautions so that only the Corn King can be injured! The winner is then allowed to start the feast and offered the choicest morsels from the table. The slain King should be either burned or buried after the feast so that he can return to the land.

To make a Corn King, take a thick bundle of straw and tie it off at one end for the head. Halfway down the bundle, split and tie to make the two legs. Across the body fix a thinner bundle to make the arms. To be traditional the 'man' should be bound with single strands of corn, but you might like to reinforce this with matching thread.

A safer version of the slaying game, suitable even for small children, is to make a small Corn King who is passed around the circle with each person taking a straw from him. The person who takes the straw which causes him to fall apart then takes the prime role in the feasting.

Gingerbread men are also traditional at this time and quite often we will actually use them as our ritual 'cakes'. These ginger biscuits in the shape of men are great fun for the youngsters, who can really get involved in decorating them with icing and small sweets.

Madron

21 September

This is the Autumn Equinox, when day and night, light and dark, are equal. It is the feast at the height of the harvest, when nearly all has been gathered in. This would have been a time of markets, festivals, processions and general gaiety. It is also known as the feast of the healer and the feast of the release of prisoners, for this is a time of year for setting aside old disputes, grudges and quarrels. Like the Spring Equinox it is a time of balance, a time to discard unwanted habits and traits and to take on new.

To Eat

Lammas and Madron have much in common from the feasting point of view, as both are festivals of the harvest, only Madron is more so! This is a time of plenty; not only is the fruit mentioned at Lammas still in season, but so too are many other foods – hops, inshore fish, oysters, game birds and meats, and vegetables such as turnip, marrow (large zucchini) and cauliflower. Many uncultivated foods grow wild and, for those who take the time to learn how to identify them, free – berries and hedgerow fruits such as blackberries, rowan, fungi of all kinds, chestnuts and hazelnuts.

This is very much the time to make the most of what is fresh and is in season. If you're not sure, cultivate your local butcher and greengrocer, who will probably be more than happy to serve you with fresh local produce rather than 'year round' imports. Buy (or borrow from your library) a good guide to field fruits, fungi, etc., and take it with you on walks to discover what is available.

Goose was the traditional meat of this season, as the geese would have been fattened on the stubble from the fields until they were large enough to feed the family. At this time of year the bird is generally smaller and less fatty than the goose of Yuletide and so does not need hot water basting, but can be simply roasted on a rack over a roasting tin (broiler tray) to catch any fat which drops. Try serving your goose with a berry sauce, perhaps cran-berries, raspberries or rowan. Vegetables should be young and fresh and only just cooked, so that they retain their crispness.

Sweet chestnuts are also coming into season at this time. These are the sort with the prickly cases. They can be peeled and eaten raw or cooked under the grill. Either way, remember to take off not only the prickly shell and hard brown inner case but also the soft velvety brown inner covering, which is quite bitter to taste. Sweet chestnuts make an excel-lent vegetable or can be added to stuffing to go with meat. Alternatively, cook and purée them before adding half their weight in sugar with a little butter to make a wonderful spread for toast or filling for meringue. It is also possible to buy tinned sweetened chestnut purée for the same purpose.

Fish and shellfish are also seasonal. Cook them simply in tinfoil with a few herbs and perhaps a little rind from a citrus fruit. Alternatively, steam them together with some finely cut vegetables and serve with boiled potatoes garnished with herb salad.

Fruit Cobbler

Make the most of the fruit available by making fruit cobbler, a blend of fresh fruit and sponge, baked in the oven.

Grease an 8-inch cake tin and then sprinkle with a good amount of sugar. Make up a standard sponge-cake mixture – 4 oz butter, 4 oz caster (granulated) sugar, 4 oz self-raising (self-rising) flour and 2 beaten eggs – and blend well until light and fluffy. Lay large pieces of fruit (with their skins if edible) and dollops of the mixture into the tin. Bake in the oven at 180°C/350°F for around 30 minutes. When it has risen and is cooked through (test with a skewer), turn out upside-down onto a plate and serve with fresh cream, crème fraîche or custard.

This is also the time of year to make jams (jellies) and preserves. A Witch of my acquaintance, with whom I frequently share a tiny kitchen, suggests that this should be included in the 'Making Merry' section, as it can easily qualify as a 'game'. Be that as it may, this is definitely the time to think about preserving the bounty of summer and autumn for the winter ahead. Make jams using traditional recipes or, rather more simply, preserve fruit between layers of sugar in strong wine or spirits.

To Drink

Fruit wines, some of which only take a few weeks to mature, are popular at this time, just as they would have been in the past. However, an even quicker alternative is to strain the juice of your favourite fruit(s) and add it to chilled sweet white wine just before serving.

Similarly, a fruit liqueur can be made by adding fruit juice and fine caster sugar to vodka. Shake well two or three times a day for a week and then serve chilled. For a non-alcoholic version, add the juice and sugar to mineral water and repeat the process.

As for Lammas, good-quality ciders and ales are very popular at this festival.

To Make Merry

We tend to think of September as the start of autumn, but it is also the tail end of summer and the weather is often still good enough to go outside, although we may have to wrap up a bit more than for previous festivals.

If you can find 'common land' which supports fruit, berries and nuts, try taking the whole family on a ramble. If you feel uncertain as to what may or may not be edible, take your field guide with you or just collect samples or make sketches of what is available to take home for identification. Either way, you will expand your knowledge of what is available in your area. Obviously you should never eat anything you are not sure of, although few poisonous species taste pleasant enough for you to persevere to the point of making yourself ill.

Horse chestnuts are readily available at this time (these have less prickly cases than the sweet variety), so revive the tradition of conker fighting. Make a hole through a nut with a skewer and suspend it on knotted string. Each combatant takes it in turn to swing their conker at their opponent's conker until one or the other breaks. This is not a game for those who don't like having their knuckles rapped by flying or loose conkers! There are reputedly many ways of enhancing your conker: soaking overnight in vinegar, polishing it with boot polish, placing it in a warm dark place for several days or preserving it from one year to the next, but for the purist all these are considered to be cheating!

Breads, Cakes and Biscuits to Honour the Goddess and the God

'Earth, my body…'

Grain, be it wheat, corn or whatever, has been planted, tended, harvested, ground and baked pretty much since man walked upright! Grain and certain forms of bread have been found in tombs dating back to the ancient Egyptians and before. The importance of this basic food is reflected in the numerous Gods and Goddesses of grain and harvest from all parts of the world and almost all stages of humanity – Attis, Ceres, Ceridwyn, Chrom Cruaich, Demeter, Dionysus, Osiris, Persephone and Robigus to name just a few – not to mention all the Gods and Goddesses of fertility whose compass includes the harvest. Bread itself has always been called the staff of life and to share bread was considered to produce social obligations on both host and guest.

Bread, biscuits (cookies) and cakes are just variations on the theme of turning ground grain into something palatable. In the Craft we have bread at all of our feasts – sometimes plain, sometimes in a special shape or with extra ingredients to remind us of the season and the stage we are at in the Wheel of the Year, sometimes just as a medium to eat with other things. We also have special biscuits (confusingly called cakes) for the Rite of Wine and Cakes, which are consecrated and shared to remind us of all the gifts of the Goddess and the God. We make other biscuits according to the season, gingerbread men for example. We eat cake itself appropriate to the season and to celebrate our Rites of Passage such as Wiccaning (the naming ritual for a child) and Handfasting (the Wiccan marriage).

Breads

Many people shrink at the idea of making their own bread, but really it is not all that complicated and the results are such an improvement on the mass-produced sliced stuff that it really is worth the effort. However, if you really don't have the time or inclination to make your own, then it is worth while cultivating a really good-quality baker's (the kind that make their own bread on the premises) and asking if they will provide you with the seasonal loaves of your choice

Bread-making is one of those tasks which are often best used as a time for meditating on the Goddess. Good bread cannot be rushed and taking your time whilst considering the fertility of the land as well as the cycle of the seasons is one way of putting the Craft into your cooking.

However, the key to making good bread lies in understanding the process by which yeast operates. Yeast is a living organism and needs to be treated in the right way for it to work properly. Fresh yeast (which can usually be obtained from a baker's shop or the bakery department of some supermarkets) needs to be really fresh – it will not keep more than a few days, or a couple of weeks in the fridge. When the time comes to use it, sprinkle it over warm water to which a little sugar has been added and give it time to become very frothy. Even dried yeast has to be 'activated' before it will work (you will find the instructions on the manufacturer's packet). Once the yeast has been added to the other ingredients and well worked in, it will need time in a warm place to rise. It will probably take about an hour to double in size. Do not be tempted to rush it – slowly-risen bread has a much better taste and texture than that which has been forced.

If you want to make sure that your bread is really good, then you will need to knead it and let it rise twice. Similarly, bread which has been kneaded lightly but well will be superior to that which has been treated with heavy hands and rushed. You are not beating it into submission, nor are you simply blending the ingredients, you are folding and kneading to let the air in.

When you first start making bread you will find that the dough sticks to your fingers. Don't worry, rub it off with a little flour and continue. To test whether bread is cooked, remove it from the tin (loaf pan) and tap it on the bottom. If cooked, it will sound hollow.

Of course you may already have your own favourite bread recipes, in which case use them, but here are two basic recipes, a simple one which is easy to shape and a wholemeal (whole-wheat) one which can be adapted to include all kinds of seasonal ingredients. I have also included a recipe for a special bread which we frequently have at our celebrations, Bara Brith.

Simple Milk Bread

This is one of the easiest bread recipes I have come across. It also lends itself to making loaves in all sorts of shapes and sizes.

½ oz fresh yeast
¼ pint tepid milk with 1 tsp sugar stirred well in
8 oz strong plain (*all-purpose*) flour
1 tsp salt
1 oz lard or margarine

Sprinkle the yeast over the milk and leave until frothy. Mix the flour and salt and rub in the fat. Add the yeast liquid and mix to a soft dough. Knead thoroughly on a floured board until smooth. Place in a bowl, cover with a slightly damp cloth and leave in a warm place (around 23°C/74°F) until doubled in size. Then knead again and leave to rise a second time. Your dough can then be divided into rolls or shaped in any way you choose. Place on a greased baking sheet (cookie sheet) and allow to rise again for another 20 minutes or so. Paint with a little milk or beaten egg and bake in the oven at 220°C/425°F for 15 to 20 minutes, depending on the thickness of your shaped loaf.

Designs for this bread include a plait or twist, a sheaf of corn for harvest time or a figure for Lammas. Consider also a spiral for Samhain (the spiral is one of the symbols of the Crone), a holly leaf for Yule, an oak leaf or the Sun for Litha, or a hare figure for Oestara.

Wholemeal Bread

¹/₄ oz fresh yeast
¹/₄ pint tepid water
¹/₂ tsp sugar
¹/₂ lb wholemeal (*wholewheat*) flour
¹/₂ tsp salt
¹/₂ oz lard

Sprinkle the yeast into the water and leave until frothy. Mix the sugar, salt and flour and rub in the fat. Add the liquid and mix to a soft dough, then turn out onto a floured surface and knead well. Place the dough into a 1 lb loaf tin, put the tin into an oiled plastic bag and place in a warm place until the dough has doubled in size. Remove from the bag and bake at 230°C/450°F for 15 minutes and then at 200°C/400°F for a further 30 minutes.

The bread can be made less dense by using a blend of 50 per cent wholemeal flour and 50 per cent strong plain (all-purpose) flour, in which case it is entirely suited to the addition of dried fruit and nuts, up to about 12 oz in total. Try dried apple and hazelnut, or sunflower and sesame seeds, dried tomato and sliced olive, or any other combination which is either seasonal or takes your fancy. The surface of your bread can also be basted with a beaten egg glaze and seeds such as poppy, sesame or caraway can be sprinkled on prior to cooking.

To go with your bread, you can choose from a huge range of things: cheeses, pâtés, meats, pastes, jams, jellies, and so on, either ready-made or home-made. For both sweet and savoury spreads try mixing a selection of ingredients into cream cheese. Curd (farmer's) cheese or mascarpone make a good base for sweet toppings. Try adding a selection of fruit and nuts, or even nuts and swirls of chocolate. Soft goat's or sheep's cheeses make a good start to more savoury ones. Add anchovies, shrimp, or small slivers of preserved meats.

A good rule of thumb when blending your own spreads is to limit the number of additional ingredients to one or two at first until you have an idea of how well they combine. Also, make small quantities and try them out. It is much better to run out of a new recipe than to end up throwing it out because it is not palatable. Remember that dried ingredients will take a few hours for their flavour to permeate into the cheese, whereas 'wet' or fresh ones will start to blend in immediately. Many shop-bought spreads will benefit from the a bit of perking up – add a teaspoonful of brandy or liqueur to any jam (jelly) and see what I mean. You can also add nuts and sliced dried fruits to preserves or a pinch of herbs to savoury jellies (*see* Chapter 11, 'Herb Sachets and Gifts', for more ideas).

Bara Brith

This very special bread should be moist and absolutely stuffed full of fruit. It really does represent the fruitfulness and bounty of the Goddess and the land. As it is so rich in itself it is generally eaten without any spreads or additions, although some butter really does complement it.

4 oz sugar
10 oz mixed dried fruit
¼ pint water
4 oz good-quality block margarine
1 tbsp treacle (*molasses*)
2 eggs
8 oz self-raising (self-rising) flour
1 tsp mixed spice

Grease a non-stick loaf tin and line with baking parchment or greaseproof paper. In a sturdy saucepan boil the sugar, fruit, margarine and water. Stir in the treacle and allow to cool slightly. Beat the eggs and add along with the flour and mixed spice. The mixture should be rather runny. Pour it into the tin and bake in the oven at 150°C/300°F for about an hour and a half. If you like a moist bread then an hour and a half may be too long, so check the bread with a skewer after one hour and again after one and a quarter hours. When the skewer comes out clean, the bread is ready. Turn it out and leave it to cool completely before serving.

Biscuits

Esbat Biscuits

These are the biscuits (cookies) that are blessed and eaten during the Rite of Wine and Cakes, the ritual celebration of the Goddess and the God which closes nearly every celebration of the Craft. They are called Esbat biscuits as the Rite which includes them usually takes place at the Esbat, or Full Moon.

There are nearly as many recipes for these biscuits that are called cakes as there are groups of Witches making them! Some traditions hold that the true Esbat biscuit will have three ingredients to represent the three aspects of the Goddess, while others feel that to truly celebrate the fertility of the land you need to have as many good things in the recipe as possible. Here are just two versions.

Simple Esbat Biscuits

3 oz caster (*granulated*) sugar
5 oz butter
7 oz plain (all-purpose) flour

Blend the butter and sugar together until pale and creamy, then work in the flour bit by bit with a fork. When you have a doughy consistency, turn out onto a very lightly floured surface and knead gently until all is evenly blended. Roll out until approx. ¼ inch thick and cut into crescent Moon shapes. If you do not have a cutter, take a small glass and cut two circles which intersect to form a crescent Moon. Place your Moons onto a greased baking sheet (cookie sheet) and cook at 150°C/300°F until lightly golden in colour. Do not overcook! If your kitchen, or your hands, are very warm, you might find it easier to chill the dough before rolling it out. If you want to 'gild the lily', try pressing a pentacle into the top of each biscuit before baking. The finished biscuits keep well in an airtight box or the dough can be frozen for future use.

Rich Esbat Biscuits

2 oz butter
1 tbsp honey
1 egg yolk
3 oz plain (*all-purpose*) flour
1 oz ground hazelnuts or almonds
a large pinch of ground cinnamon
a large pinch of grated nutmeg
a few drops of vanilla essence or extract

Blend the butter, honey, vanilla and egg yolk together until you have a thick paste. Mix all the dried ingredients together and add to the paste a little at a time until you have a stiff dough. Chill slightly, then roll and cut out as before. Cook on a greased baking sheet at 160°C/325°F until pale golden (about 15 minutes).

You can vary this recipe with a little grated chocolate and some desiccated coconut (coconut flakes) or press chopped nuts into the surface just before baking.

These biscuits can also be made in shapes appropriate to the Sabbats if you have either the patience to cut them out by hand or can find pastry cutters in appropriate shapes. Try a holly leaf for Yule, candles or hares for Imbolg, and so on.

Fortune Meringues

These biscuits are especially good for the times of year when divination is appropriate, Beltane and Samhain in particular. First you will need to decide what symbols or messages you are going to hide within the meringue and mark them onto either rice paper (which can be eaten) or greaseproof paper (in which case caution your guests not to eat it!) You might like to go for Craft-related symbols: a broomstick (for travel), a cauldron (wisdom), a sheaf of corn (wheat) (fertility), and so on. Alternatively, use more 'orthodox' symbols such as linked rings (for romance) or a letter (news), or choose quotations or sayings – really it is up to you. You can either make a note of the meanings you have assigned to the symbols or you can enjoy the fun as people try to work out their own interpretations. Roll each 'motto' into a small tight curl and then you are ready to make your meringues.

2 egg whites
4 oz caster (*granulated*) sugar

Line a baking sheet (cookie sheet) with non-stick paper and warm the oven to 130°C/250°F. Beat the egg whites until very stiff – a balloon whisk is best, if a bit tiring. Then add half the sugar and whisk again until once more very stiff. Fold the remaining sugar in with a metal spoon, being careful not to knock the air out of the egg whites. Place thin circles of meringue onto the baking sheet, place each 'motto' carefully onto the centre, then top with a small dollop of meringue. Cook slowly for 1 to 2 hours, being careful not to let them go brown.

As these will be very sweet, make them as small as possible and perhaps provide a citrus sauce for dipping.

Gingerbread Men

Lammas is the traditional time for gingerbread men. You can usually buy them in the shops nearly all year round, but you will find that most of these are very hard (they need to be in order to have a repeatable shape). Try making your own using the Simple Esbat Biscuits recipe (*above*), to which you add 1 to 2 tsps of ground ginger.

Cakes

Cakes form the centrepiece of all celebrations from a child's first birthday to the grandest many-tiered wedding cake. They come in all shapes, sizes and colours and with all kinds of decoration. If you're serious about cake-making then there are many excellent books you can take your inspiration from. If, however, you want to stay in the realm of the gifted amateur, then perhaps these recipes will give you some ideas to work with.

Basic Sponge Cake

This recipe is the starting-point for many cakes.

4 oz butter
4 oz caster (*granulated*) sugar
2 beaten eggs
4 oz self-raising (*self-rising*) flour

Cream the butter and sugar together, beat in the eggs, stir in the flour. Turn into a greased and floured 8-inch tin or individual baking cases. Bake at 180°C/350°F for 25 to 35 minutes. Test with a skewer to see whether it is done (if a skewer comes out clean, the cake is cooked).

This recipe can form a basis for any number of variations. Try:

cocoa powder and chocolate chips
ground coconut and white chocolate buttons
mixed spice and dried fruit
a few drops of almond essence and chopped nuts

You can use any combination you like really, only make sure that wet ingredients are added at the same time as the egg and chunky dry ones (dried fruit or nuts) are rolled in the flour and then added with it.

Once the cake is cooked, you can decorate it with icing, pieces of dried fruit, curls of chocolate or anything that takes your fancy. If you're looking for something a bit more original, try adding a few strands of saffron to your cake mix and decorating with fresh mint leaves. Alternatively, fill individual cake cases a third full and add a small drop of apricot jam with a sprinkling of chopped nuts before topping up with some more cake mix. Try to ensure that the raw ingredients do not come up farther than two thirds of the case to allow for rising.

Individual cakes are great for feasting and seasonal celebrations as they can be decorated to match the event – a miniature chocolate egg for Oestara, black icing in the shape of a bat or black cat for Samhain, and so on.

Chocolate Brownies

These rich nutty brownies are one of those treats that you don't need to worry about storing – they rarely last that long!

3 oz butter
2 oz plain (semi-sweet) chocolate
6 oz caster (*granulated*) sugar
2½ oz self-raising (*self-rising*) flour
a generous pinch of salt
2 eggs beaten with ½ tsp vanilla essence (*extract*)
4 oz chopped mixed nuts

Melt the butter and chocolate in a basin over hot water and add the sugar. Sift the flour and salt, stir in the nuts, add the chocolate mixture and then the eggs. Beat until well mixed and pour into a greased and floured 8-inch square baking tin. Bake at 180°C/350°F for about 35 minutes, testing with a skewer after about 25 minutes. Do not allow it to get too dark.

Biscuit Cake

No cooking is required for this one and it is a great favourite with the young.

8 oz crushed digestive biscuits (*Graham crackers*)
4 oz butter
4 oz (light) brown sugar
4 oz mixed chopped nuts
2 oz sultanas (*seedless raisins, white or golden*)
8 oz good-quality chocolate

Melt the butter, sugar and 3 oz chocolate in a pan, add the crushed biscuits and nuts, and stir really well. Press down really firmly into a loose-bottomed greased tin and chill for a couple of hours. Once it has set hard, remove from the tin (a palette-knife dipped into hot water helps with this) and place on a plate. Melt the remaining chocolate in a bowl sitting in a pan of hot water and pour over the cake. Smooth it out with the palette-knife. Before the chocolate sets, mark it into slices, then chill it again.

Celebration Cakes

As with almost every other tradition or belief system, decorated cakes are the centrepiece of the Witches' festivities. Most commonly thought of is the wedding cake, but there are also cakes to celebrate the birth of a child, the coming of age of a youngster and significant birthdays. It is not necessary to stick to current trends – i.e. you do not have to have a many-tiered rich fruitcake covered with rock-hard white icing to celebrate a wedding, or Handfasting as it is known in the Craft. You can opt for something lighter and if only having one layer, you can shape and decorate it in any number of ways. My own Handfasting cake was a horseshoe-shaped light sponge with a Maypole in the centre, decorated with flowers and in the colours of the Goddess and the God at Beltane.

There are a number of ways of approaching the celebration cake – buying it ready-made, getting a confectioner to make it especially for you, buying a ready-made cake and shaping and decorate it yourself or making it yourself from first principles. The latter option is the most satisfying, but also the most time-consuming, and if you are not naturally artistic then you may find that it is also the most stressful. Having said that, it is generally worth putting at least some of the effort in yourself if you can.

When planning a celebration cake, think ahead:

★ First you need at least some idea of how many people you expect to share the cake, as you want neither to run out nor to be eating it yourself for the next month. And whilst you're thinking about size, remember to spare a thought for what you intend to put your finished cake onto!

★ Secondly, if the celebration is not taking place in your home, then you need to ensure that you can safely transport the cake or finish its assembly at the location of the party.

★ Thirdly, give yourself enough time. Even the simplest cake is best produced over two days – one to make and cool the cake and the second to decorate it – and if you are involved in any other way with the party arrangements then neither of those two days should be the day of the celebration.

★ The last major part of the planning should be to design your cake. Give some thought as to the interests of the person, or people, it is intended for. Dracula rising from his coffin with a lot of black, brown and purple icing is not everyone's idea of something they actually want to eat! It's also worth bearing in mind that children's cakes are often better without a lot of colourings and added flavourings, as their bodies are often not developed enough to cope with artificial ingredients, and the result can be a roomful of hyperactive youngsters!

★ Finally work out exactly what ingredients and decorations you are going to need and check that you have everything in stock. There's nothing as irritating as discovering that you don't quite have enough icing sugar or that you lent your best tin to someone who has yet to return it!

Cake Design

Cake design is not as complicated as most people think. First sketch out your idea on paper, then reduce that design to a series of basic shapes, squares, rectangles, circles and triangles. All these are shapes that can be easily cut from a flat sponge cake. A light fruit-cake can also be used, but will be harder to shape because of the bits of fruit in it. When it comes to sticking the shapes together, sieved apricot or strawberry jam (jelly) is usually the best. Don't forget to leave room for a layer of some kind of filling – cream and jam, but-tercream, etc. The cake can then be iced, either using shop-bought flat icing or your own home-made.

If you find yourself short of ideas, have a good look at the cakes on sale in most large supermarkets or be a bit cheeky and go into a baker's which does made-to-order cakes and have a look through their book of suggested designs.

Some Celebration Cake Ideas

★ *Handfasting* (*Wedding*): Horseshoe, bell(s) or, if you're feeling humorous, try a double bed! Something less obvious is to make a light sponge cake full of dried and glazed fruit and to bake it in a ring mould (tube pan). The finished cake is then decorated with more glazed fruit and even flowers. Those who wish to be really symbolic can make two rings and link them by cutting and sticking with jam or jelly.

★ *Naming* (*Christening*): Teddy bear, duck, rabbit or any other 'stuffed toy' theme. A baby in a crib – make the crib from two oblong cakes trimmed to fit, dress the bed with icing bedclothes and place a marzipan baby under an icing quilt. A more interesting version of this is to create a 'nursery' on the top of a flat cake. Provide a crib and baby, a dresser or chest of drawers (look in toy shops for low-cost doll's house furniture), then make some miniature clothes and toys from marzipan and scatter them around. If you are feeling really competent, make a packet of nappies (diapers), wipes, etc.

★ *Coming of Age*: Here you really do need some idea of the teenager's interests and of the sort of person they are. Often teenagers feel more comfortable with something shop-bought anyway. Sports themes are the easiest, as you can use a basic oblong to represent the field and make figures from marzipan in the appropriate costumes or colours. Alternatively, if they have a career in mind, think of something along those lines. Whatever you do, remember that it is best to err on the side of being too adult rather than choosing something twee or childish.

★ *Retirement*: Here you should be able to choose from a number of themes as older people tend to be more open about what interests them. Take some time in the months before the event to have a sneaky look on their bookshelves or at any magazines they may read and try to find out what kind of TV programmes they watch. All this may provide ideas. If you are stuck, think about making a cake in the shape of an armchair, perhaps with a folded newspaper on the arm, or, for someone who thinks work was a bit of a grind, make a basic-shaped cake and place a pair of handcuffs and a bolt cutter on the top!

★ **Withdrawal (Death):** Many people find it hard to be celebratory about the passing of a loved one, however this is an excellent time to celebrate their achievements and the things they have brought to those around them. If you can, try to incorporate one or more of these themes in the cake. If your loved one had a sense of humor you can try to reflect this, but do be careful, emotions are always high at this time and offence can be easily taken. For some reason it seems that the 'default setting' for most people on this occasion is the Black Forest gâteau. I have no idea why, but if, like me, you find this totally inappropriate, perhaps you might like to try baking a cake of the kind that person liked in their lifetime and finding a photo of them, preferably at their best, and simply placing the picture on top of the cake.

★ *Other Celebrations:*

★ *Passing exams:* Try a pile of books with a 'diploma' on top

★ *Passing a driving test:* A steering wheel

★ *Return from a long journey:* A passport accompanied by items symbolic
of the places visited
★ *Return from hospital:* A bedpan!

★ *Recovery from illness:* Try making a series of empty medicine bottles and pill packets

★ *Birthdays in general:* The person's interests, or be humorous and make something
which reflects whatever they've been talking most about recently!

★ *New job:* Something indicative of the nature of the job or, more simply,
a wallet with money sticking out (use toy money for speed and simplicity)

If you find yourself enjoying the idea of theme cakes but don't have a suitable date coming up, you can always take a leaf from Winnie the Pooh and have an 'unbirthday'. As Pooh says, you can have up to 364 of these most years and 365 in a leap year!

Soups and Foods to Strengthen and Heal

'To heal their bodies and make their spirits whole...'

Just about everyone is familiar with the Jewish stereotype of some nice chicken soup to make the patient feel better. But this is more than just a humorous comment on Jewish mothers – it used to be common for special foods to be recommended for different ailments. This is not only because food is nourishing, and therefore necessary to healing, but also because different foods have different properties, both physical and Magical. Not only that, but if you're feeling under the weather or down in the dumps then some freshly and lovingly prepared food will often make you feel a lot better.

These days we eat far too many pre-packaged and instant meals full of chemical additives, flavourings and colours, and miss out on the joy of natural foods. Even if you do have a hectic life, it is well worth treating yourself to a freshly cooked meal as often as you can. I know that it's so much easier to grab a piece of cheese from the fridge or shove something in the microwave (and it saves on the washing up), but good food, well prepared and nicely presented, is not only good for the body, it inspires the spirit too.

One of the keys to feeding the poorly is to make food look and smell appetizing. Another important tip is to serve small portions, there is nothing so offputting as being confronted with a huge amount of food when your appetite needs stimulating.

Soups

I have emphasized soups in the title of this chapter not only because soup is easily swallowed and digested, but also because it lends itself easily to variations, allowing you to select different herbs and spices for their healing properties. Contrary to most people's expectations, soup is surprisingly easy to make from raw ingredients and the home-made variety is so much nicer than the kind you get in cans and packets.

The key to good soup lies in the stock (broth) you use. You can either make your own from first principles – boiling bones with a little meat left on them in water to which you have added a small chopped carrot, a small chopped onion and a bouquet garni, or making a vegetable stock and straining it well – or you can use stock cubes. If you choose the latter, make sure they are good-quality stock cubes, not simply flavouring cubes. The better varieties tend to call themselves bouillon cubes and because they are made from real ingredients tend to have a slightly greasy and granular feel to them when crumbled. Try to stay away from the ones which look and feel a bit like compressed tobacco! It is a good idea when trying out a new brand to actually taste the stock before you add it to your ingredients, that way you will know just how much flavour it has. If your soup has well-flavoured ingredients, you can use plain water with a small amount of salt rather than stock.

You don't need a lot of specialist equipment to make soup, but a good-sized heavy saucepan with a lid is useful. If you have a pressure cooker this is excellent, not so much for actually pressure cooking your soup, as you do not want to cook at pressure for more than two to five minutes, but because of its size, weight and well-fitting lid. When it comes to blending your soup, either use a hand blender or push the soup through a coarse sieve. Try to avoid the kind of electric blender which reduces everything to a pulp. Soup with texture is far more interesting than soup which is like a thin gravy!

Those of you who feel that the quantities given below are too large can always scale down, but do remember that soup freezes really well. One of the best methods is to place a freezer bag inside a small freezer-proof bowl or cup and fill with the amount of soup that makes a portion, and repeat as necessary until you have portioned down all your soup. Seal the bag(s) and place them, still in the container(s), in the freezer. Once frozen, the container(s) can be removed and you will have individual portions of soup ready to hand. Remember to label your soups, as they tend to look much of a muchness when frozen.

Basic Soup

To my way of thinking the number one basic soup recipe is potato and onion soup. It's quick, easy and provides the base for any number of variations.

3 pints water or chicken stock (*broth*) (*if using water add ¹/₂ tsp salt*)
1 lb peeled chopped potatoes
1 lb peeled chopped onions
1 tsp parsley

Place all the ingredients in a large saucepan, bring to the boil and simmer for 20 minutes. Either mix using a hand blender or push through a coarse sieve. Serve.

Potato and onion soup is good for strengthening the immune system and stimulating the appetite.

To this basic recipe can be added any number of vegetables and herbs in almost any combination you can think of. Try some of the following:

a good head of broccoli and 2 oz blue cheese
(cheese generally needs to be added at the end of cooking)
1 lb parsnip and 1 tsp curry powder
1 lb diced carrots and 2 tbsps dried red lentils
a handful of peeled boiled chestnuts and 2 tbsps sweetcorn (*corn*)

If you chill the basic potato and onion soup and add ¹/₂ pint cream and ¹/₂ tsp salt, you have an excellent quick vichyssoise.

Hearty Soups

Hearty soups are really just those which are a bit thicker and have recognizable chunks of meat and/or vegetables in them. Take the basic recipe, increase the amount of potato and blend less thoroughly, or remove half the cooked vegetables with a slotted spoon, blend the remainder, then add back the solid pieces. The texture you are aiming for is something between a soup and a stew.

Sweetcorn Chowder

Sweetcorn chowder is a variation on this theme. It is hearty soup full of vitamins and minerals, tasty and colourful enough to tempt the most tired palate.

2 potatoes
1 onion
1 tin of drained sweetcorn (*corn*)
1 tin of tomatoes
2 pints of water
1 tbsp cornflower (*corn-starch*)
¹/₂ pint milk

Peel and dice the potatoes and the onion. Place them, together with the sweetcorn and tomatoes, in the water, bring to the boil and simmer for 15 minutes. Add the cornflour to the milk, blend well and add to the soup. Warm through until the cornflour has thickened and serve.

Chilli Soup

Similar to chilli con carne, this helps to clear congestion and drive away colds and 'flu.

¹/₂ lb beef mince (*ground beef*)
2 sliced onions
2 small finely chopped chilli peppers
2 sliced cloves of garlic
1 large sliced red pepper
3 tsps paprika powder
1 tin of kidney beans
1 tin of tomatoes
1 pint of water

Fry the mince and the onions (without any added fat) until the mince is fully cooked. Add the chilli peppers, garlic and red pepper and cook gently for a further 5 minutes. Add the paprika, kidney beans, tomatoes and water. Bring to the boil and simmer for 15 minutes.

Clear Soups

In a clear soup you are aiming for a clear liquid in which the ingredients are suspended. As an alternative to water you can always use equal amounts of tinned consommé and water. Probably the best known clear soup is French onion soup. This version is excellent for sore throats and warding off the symptoms of a head cold.

French Onion Soup

2 lb chopped onions
1 oz butter
2 pints beef stock (*bouillon broth*)
(*vegetarians can use vegetable stock plus ¹/₂ tsp yeast extract*)
1 or 2 chopped cloves of garlic
freshly ground black pepper

Cook the onions gently in the butter until golden brown. This takes around 20 minutes, but watch and stir regularly. Add the beef stock, garlic and a good quantity of the black pepper. Bring to the boil, cover and simmer for around 20 minutes. If you have the time, allow the soup to rest for at least an hour then warm it through. This helps the flavours to merge thoroughly.

Cream of Cheddar Soup

To turn onion soup into a meal on its own, try cream of cheddar soup. You will need:

several slices of lightly toasted bread
sliced cheddar cheese

Layer the bread and cheese upright in a casserole dish (it helps to tilt the dish). One the dish is loosely packed, add onion soup until the dish is about two thirds full, then bake in a moderate oven (175°C/350°F) for about 30 minutes.

This is an excellent winter warmer as well as helping to ward off colds and 'flu.

Other variations on the above onion soup include:

Spicy Mushroom

Use ½ lb of thinly sliced mushrooms and a small chilli pepper instead of the onion.

Sweetcorn and Egg

Use chicken stock (broth), 1 thinly sliced onion and 3 tbsps sweetcorn to make the soup and when it is cooked thoroughly beat 2 eggs, stir them quickly into the soup and cook. They will form thin strands.

Chilled Soups

Chilled soups tend to have less texture and so will need more blending. As they are chilled they will also need a little more salt, so if you sample them before chilling they should taste slightly salty. Quite a few people have a reluctance to try chilled soup, believing that it is going to taste strange, but as my mother used to say, 'You can't tell me you don't like it if you haven't tried it!'

Cucumber Soup

This one is really easy to make and has a wonderful delicate flavour. Cucumber is known for cooling and cleansing the blood and bringing about a clear complexion.

1 thinly chopped onion
1 thinly chopped clove of garlic
1 oz butter
1 peeled and thinly sliced cucumber
2 tsps parsley
1 pint water
¼ to ½ tsp salt
½ pint milk

Fry the onion and the garlic gently in the butter until the onion is clear but not coloured. Add the cucumber, parsley, salt and water and cook gently for about 10 minutes. Blend really well and then add the milk. Sample to see if you can taste the salt. Allow to cool then chill in the fridge for 1 hour.

Carrot, Orange and Coriander Soup

This soup is a great energy-giver, whether on the physical or Magical plane. It is excellent for use before solar or power rituals.

1 lb thinly sliced carrots
1 thinly sliced onion
¹/₂ oz butter
1 pint water
1 tsp crushed coriander seeds
juice of 4 large oranges (*or ¹/₂ pint fresh orange juice if you're really short of time!*)
thinly sliced rind of 1 orange

Fry the carrots and onion gently in the butter for around 10 minutes. Add the water and coriander seeds, bring to the boil and simmer gently for 15 minutes. Blend really thoroughly. Add the orange juice and rind. Cook gently for a further 5 minutes (do not allow to boil) and taste to see whether it needs salt. Cool thoroughly and chill for at least an hour before serving.

Presentation

As mentioned earlier, food for the poorly, and indeed anyone, should always be well presented. Use attractive china, provide a serviette, and perhaps put a flower beside the place setting.

Another way of enhancing the look of food is to garnish it. A sprig of fresh herb, a curl of fruit rind or a swirl of cream can make all the difference to the appearance of a soup.

Croutons, whether made from fried or toasted bread, also look good and they add texture to a dish. Try to make your own, as the ready-made ones can sometimes be rock hard. Fried croutons may not sound very health-giving, but if you melt a little butter with some fresh herbs and garlic and allow it to steep for 5 – 10 minutes then you are adding the goodness of these seasonings to your dish.

Butter, by the way, is not as unhealthy as the advertisers would have you believe – it contains vitamins A and D and comes from a natural source. A thin scrape of butter may well contain less cholesterol than a thick layer of many other spreads. Of course some fresh bread with real butter is tempting, too. Have a look at some of the ideas in Chapter 7, 'Breads, Cakes and Biscuits to Honour the Goddess and the God'.

Alternatively, try a small side plate of fresh salad. These days there is no reason why salad should just be the plain (and somewhat boring) cucumber, lettuce and tomato. Most supermarkets stock ready-to-eat mixed-leaf salads and you can add slices of melon, orange or any other fruit or vegetable, or herbs. Cubes of cheese, slices of boiled (hard-cooked) egg, small pieces of well-crisped bacon, sesame or sunflower seeds and pine nuts all make interesting additions to salad.

One of my favourite salad recipes is to slice a couple of fresh vine tomatoes, sprinkle with freshly ground salt and black pepper, and leave for at least five minutes before serving with a little cubed feta or other strong cheese.

Other Dishes

Soups are not the only way of providing health-giving nourishment – the same herbs, vegetables and so on can be eaten on their own or added to almost any other kind of dish. In cold weather casseroles and stews are good candidates. In warmer weather you might like to think about making quiches or small pies and pastries (see later in this chapter for some recipes). Add herbs, raw or partly cooked vegetables and fruit to salads, and have a look at the herb jellies later in the chapter. Use your imagination to create as many new recipes as you can.

Just Potatoes

This is one of the most flexible recipes I have found. It also has the advantage of using up leftovers.

1 or 2 potatoes per person
1 egg per potato
pieces of finely chopped cooked meats, tuna, cheese(s),
vegetables, herbs and spices to taste

Scrub the potatoes well and bake them in their skins in the microwave or conventional oven until cooked through. Halve and carefully scoop out the flesh, leaving the skins intact. Mix the flesh in a bowl with 1 beaten egg per potato, together with your chosen added ingredients. Blend the mixture well and pile back into the skins (it will be quite a bit higher than the level of the skins). Bake in a medium-hot oven (190 – 200°C/375 – 400°F) for about 20 minutes and serve with spicy sauce, mayonnaise or chutney.

The Properties of Some Foods

We all know that vegetables are good for us. They contain high vitamin, mineral and fibre content. But they also have other effects on us. These qualities used to be well known but have been largely relegated to folklore and myth. The following is not meant to be a comprehensive list but enough to give you some idea of properties that used to be associated with the plants that we eat.

★ *Asparagus*: This has a high mineral content and is said to have aphrodisiac properties.

★ *Black Pepper*: Penetrating and stimulating, black pepper is said to make it easier to absorb other nutrients.

★ *Carrot*: Carrot contains plenty of vitamin A, which, I regret to say, does not really help you see in the dark. It does, however, enable to the body to repair itself.

Be careful not to take in too much vitamin A (or for that matter too much of many other vitamins), though, as it can cause problems.

★ *Chocolate*: Chocolate contains a chemical similar to that produced by the brain when in love, hence its use in comforting someone who has been rejected by a lover. The other good news is that a small amount of chocolate is supposed to be good for the heart as well as provide a source of iron.

★ *Coriander*: Coriander is a stimulating herb, although too much can make you sleepy. The seeds were considered by the Chinese to confer immortality.

★ *Garlic*: Purifying, supports the immune system.

★ *Onion*: Strengthening and purifying, helps to fight off infections and disease.

★ *Parsley*: This is known for its healing properties as well as its ability to remove poisons and negativity.

★ *Potato*: A good source of vitamin C, the potato was also thought to be of benefit in reducing rheumatism and indeed science is now finding that this may be more than just folklore.

★ *Rosemary*: Rosemary was considered to represent fidelity between lovers and was often worn by the bride at weddings. It has long been used as an incense, not only to honour the Gods but also to aid healing. The leaves were felt to dispel bad dreams and to aid mental powers. Oil of rosemary is useful in curing headaches and a tea made from the leaves will help with all kinds of digestive upset.

★ *Sage*: This was believed to be good for the head and to quicken the intellect. It also makes an excellent mouthwash, soothing all kinds of throat infections and helping to strengthen the gums. Sage tea will help to reduce fevers and is also useful in cleansing skin wounds.

★ *Spinach*: Best known for its high levels of iron, spinach also contains high levels of chlorophyll, which also helps 'strengthen' the blood and vitamin D. Spinach was believed to be an all-round mental and physical tonic and stimulant.

★ *Thyme*: Thyme was used as a symbol of activity, bravery and energy. It was used in the treatment of uterine disorders, including painful periods. Additionally it can help with digestive and respiratory problems.

Foods of Love

One category of food which deserves a special mention is that chosen to enhance a romantic mood. As a romantic meal can be anything from a candlelit supper to a picnic, this covers quite a lot of ground. However, there are some principles which hold true in most cases and some foods which definitely have romantic associations.

First, it is important to have the right atmosphere. A romantic picnic will be spoiled if the ground is soggy and the air full of insects, just as a more formal dinner will be spoilt if there are dirty socks or children's toys scattered about the floor. Having said that, however, any partner or potential partner who can't laugh away the inconveniences of real life is someone you might want to think twice about!

The next thing you need to bear in mind is that a romantic tryst is something which requires both parties to be present, rather than one of them being welded to the stove, red in the face and worrying about whether the soufflé will turn out well! Above all, this is not the time to try new and complicated recipes which you may not even like. So think of dishes which require little attention and prepare as much as you can in advance so that you have time to relax and enjoy the other person's company.

Also, try to avoid things that are difficult to eat or that are likely to get stuck in the teeth. Spaghetti is one of those dishes which some people just can't eat without getting it all over their clothes and there's no need to embarrass your guest if you're not sure they've got the knack. Similarly, whilst corn on the cob laced with butter tastes wonderful, it does have a tendency to leave bits between the teeth and butter all over the chin!

Of course finger foods can be very romantic, especially if you share them from the same dish. Try putting out a selection of bite-sized nibbles – small pies, open sandwiches, spiced chicken drumsticks, cream cheese and herb balls, fingers of carrot, baby sweetcorn and an assortment of dips – and take it in turns to feed each other. Put everything out together and have a finger bowl, with a slice of lemon and perhaps some rose petals floating in it, and some table napkins, so that fingers can be cleaned.

Another thing to remember is that small amounts of food beautifully presented are much better than a huge blow-out that leaves either one or both parties so full that they feel anything but romantic. One idea that I have found works really well is to work out a menu composed almost entirely of starters: soup, a seafood dish, salad, a platter of ribs in sauce, a light dessert, some cheese and fresh fruit.

The list of foods with a romantic or aphrodisiac reputation is quite lengthy, but here are some you might want to try:

★ Asparagus spears served with melted butter.

★ Eels cooked in white wine and cream. Get your fishmonger to gut, skin and cut them into bite-sized pieces for you. Almost all seafood and shellfish have a good reputation for being aphrodisiac, and their lightness of texture certainly fulfils one of the main criteria for a romantic food.

★ Fresh figs – cut a cross from the top nearly all the way to the base and open them out slightly.

★ Steak, whilst said to feed passion, is probably best left for meals out as it requires you to be in the kitchen cooking it, not enjoying the company.

★ Garlic is a great aphrodisiac, but make sure that you both eat it, otherwise the abstainer will almost certainly smell it on the person who did partake.

Some Romantic Recipes

As one of the essentials to a romantic evening at home is not to spend too much time in the kitchen the following recipes can all be prepared in advance to the point marked (^).

Garlic Soup

This is not as strong-tasting as you might think – in fact many people cannot even tell what it is made from.

4 to 5 uncut peeled cloves of garlic
½ tsp salt
1 clove
a pinch each of sage, thyme and parsley (*or a fresh sprig of the latter if you can*)
1 pint of water
1 tbsp olive oil
1 egg yolk

Take the garlic, olive oil, salt, clove, sage, thyme, parsley and water, bring to the boil and simmer for 30 minutes. Strain then crush the garlic cloves back into the liquid. Beat the egg yolk until thick and then beat in the olive oil drop by drop (^). Just before serving, warm the soup and beat a tablespoonful into the egg mixture, then add the rest of the soup, beating vigorously all the time. Serve immediately with small circles of hard toast and grated fresh Parmesan.

Avocado Prawn

Not the prawn cocktail nestling in the centre of half an avocado, but a more elegant version!

Peel and thinly slice the avocado and arrange half in a fan on each plate. Buy the largest prawns you can afford, Tiger prawns are great and you'll only need 3 to 4 per person. Arrange these to one side of the fan. Make your own dipping sauce from either 2 tbsps mayonnaise, 1 tsp salad cream and ¹/₂ tsp tomato purée or from 3 tbsps mayonnaise and 1 crushed clove of garlic. Put a good-sized spoonful at the base of the fan. In the empty quarter of each plate put a couple of teaspoons of lumpfish roe (or real caviar if you can afford it). (^) Serve with plenty of fresh bread available on the table.

Scampi in Love

1 small onion
1 oz butter
8 oz scampi
1 tbsp Pernod
1 tsp brandy
1 egg yolk
¹/₄ pint double (*heavy*) cream

Thinly slice the onion and lightly cook in the butter until it is soft and transparent. Add the scampi and cook gently until it has just changed from translucent to pale pink (^). Add the Pernod and brandy and continue to cook for a further 2 to 3 minutes. Mix the egg yolk and cream and stir into the pan. Continue to heat slowly, stirring all the time, until the sauce thickens. Serve with fresh crusty bread and a light salad of mixed leaves.

Champagne Scallops

6 scallops
1 tsp mixed breadcrumbs and grated Parmesan
sparkling dry wine (*or champagne*)

Take the scallops and clean them thoroughly, removing any gritty black bits (^). Cook gently in 3 tbsps sparkling dry wine (or champagne) for 5 to 7 minutes, depending on size. Arrange in two heatproof dishes, top with the mixed breadcrumbs and grated Parmesan and place under a hot grill until they start to brown. Just before serving add 1 tsp of sparkling wine to each dish (carefully as the cold wine may spit on hitting the hot dish) and serve with Melba toast. Melba toast can be approximated by taking thinly sliced bread with the crusts removed and cooking it under a hot grill on one side only so that it curls. It is allowed to become completely cold before eating.

Hot Chicken Salad

2 – 4 rashers of bacon
1 oz butter
1/2 clove crushed garlic
1 tsp chopped parsley
2 small chicken breasts
mixed salad leaves

Grill the bacon until very crisp, put to one side to cool, then break it into small pieces. Mix the butter with the garlic and parsley and use this to butter 2 slices of bread on both sides, then cook quickly in a frying pan (skillet) until golden on both sides. Cut into cubes and put aside to cool. Make a mixed-leaf salad with a couple of varieties of lettuce, watercress, etc. All this can be prepared well in advance, the day before if you like (^).

Grill the chicken breasts until cooked all the way through (about 7 to 10 minutes per side). Whilst they are cooking, mix together the salad leaves and add the cubed toast and crisped bacon. Pile onto two plates. Slice the chicken breasts immediately, creating short thin bite-sized strips, and lay them on top of the salad. Serve with a dribble of hollandaise sauce or garlic mayonnaise.

Mini Pies

There is something about home-baked pies which has a romance of its own – perhaps it's the thought of someone making and rolling out pastry just for you. Having said that, I must confess that I rarely make pastry from first principles. I find it so much quicker to buy frozen and work from that and the results are nearly as good.

The secret to good pies lies in the size and the fillings. If you're making them as 'finger food' then you won't be putting much more than a teaspoonful of filling in your pastry and hence need a square or circle only about 4 to 6 inches across. Roll your pastry as thin as you dare, certainly less than 1/4 inch thick, and then allow it to rest laid over the rolling pin for a good 10 minutes. This is because it needs to 'relax' before you put the filling in, otherwise the pastry may shrink and the pie open in the oven. Place a teaspoon of your chosen filling in the centre and then bind the edges together with a little beaten egg and a pinching motion with your fingertips. Make a small hole in the top of each pie with a skewer or pointed knife and then glaze with a light brushing of beaten egg. Cook the pies on a greased baking sheet for about 15 to 20 minutes in a preheated oven around 175°C/350°F.

If you want to give your pastry a personal touch, roll it out very thinly then layer in a few pinches of herbs, some paprika or some grated cheese. Then fold over and roll out again.

For fillings you can have any number of things, but you might like to try:

★ sheep's cheese mixed with a pinch of dill
★ cooked white fish and sliced mushroom
★ cream cheese and chopped peeled tomato
★ chopped boiled egg, parsley and cooked fish
★ minced cooked lamb with slivers of garlic and rosemary
★ sliced cooked chicken with walnuts and spring onions (scallions or green onions)
★ grated cheddar, sliced mushroom and pine nuts

You can also use your imagination when shaping pies. Try:

★ crescents, by folding a circle in half
★ mini-pasties, again using a circle, but this time bringing both sides up over the centre
★ domes – here you take a pinch of pastry from the circle and bring it up over the centre, then the piece next to it so that they overlap. Move all the way around the circle and finally give the centre point a twist. From a pastry square you can bring the four corners together in the centre to make a squared dome.

Of course the pies themselves can be decorated with pastry leaves or flowers stuck on with a little beaten egg. Perhaps sprinkle some poppy, sesame or caraway seeds on just after glazing. Another variation on this theme is mini-savoury, or sweet, tarts. For these you will need a circular pastry-cutter – the kind used for making jam tarts (jelly tarts) is ideal – and a baking tin of the kind used for making small cakes. Grease the tin well, cut the pastry into circles and place a circle in each place. Fill to about two thirds with your chosen mixture and bake for about 15 minutes.

Pies can also be made using shortcrust, puff or even filo (phyllo) pastry (use two or three sheets' thickness). Tarts don't really work with puff pastry, as it expands too much. The variations and permutations are endless, so let your imagination take hold of you (^).

Once cooked, both pies and tarts will usually keep for three or four days in an airtight tin and can be gently reheated in the oven for about five minutes. Do not try to reheat them in the microwave, as it makes the pastry soggy.

It is a good idea to serve mini-pies with a selection of chutneys or pickles, some fruity, some spicy.

Elderflower and Rose Petal Jelly

Make up 1/2 pint jelly from plain gelatine and either elderflower wine or diluted elderflower cordial. Pour into wine glasses with 6 – 8 rose petals in each and chill until set. You will probably find that you make more than 2 glassfuls, but you can always save some for another day. If you wish, serve with a dollop of crème fraîche on the top (^).

Chocolate-Dipped Fruit

Strawberries, seedless grapes, apricots, plums and many other fruits can be half dipped in melted chocolate which is allowed to set before serving. Some of the fruit can also be dipped into caster (granulated) sugar before the chocolate sets (^).

Chocolate Fondue

A variation on this is a chocolate fondue. Melt good-quality chocolate, cream and a couple of toffees (or use toffee chocolate bars) in a small fondue and serve with bite-sized pieces of fruit.

Herb Jellies, Vinegars and Oils

As well as being added directly to dishes, all kinds of herbs and spices can be used to flavour sauces, chutneys, dressings, sweet and savoury jellies to add to your food.

Oils and Vinegars

Oils and vinegars are very simple to prepare, although it is important to start with the best oil or vinegar that you can afford, as a poor base will affect the taste of your finished product. Select the herbs that you want to add, choose attractive-looking bits of the plant, wash and dry them carefully, and if they are dense or woody, bruise them slightly. Remove a little oil from the bottle and add the herbs, reseal and label the bottle carefully. Leave in a dark place at room temperature for about three months, then sample. If the flavour is not strong enough, reseal and leave a bit longer.

Jellies are an old-fashioned but really tasty way of adding to basic foods and are not as difficult to make as most people think. Here is a basic recipe and some suggestions for variants and uses.

Apple-and Jelly

3 lb cooking apples
¹/₂ pint water
2 lb sugar
herbs and flavourings to taste

Peel, core and slice the cooking apples and place into a large heavy-based saucepan with the water. Add about a handful of whatever other herbs and flavourings you choose. Simmer very gently until all the apples are soft. Add the sugar and stir until dissolved. Bring to the boil until setting point is reached. Place a little on a cold saucer and when cool, tilt to see if a skin has formed. Put through a strainer to remove any pieces. The more carefully you strain, the clearer your jelly will be. If you do not strain the mixture you will have something approaching chutney. Pour into sterile jars (see p.16 for advice on sterilizing jars), cover with a small circle of waxed paper and when cool cover with cellophane and label.

To this basic recipe you can add almost anything you can think of, for example:

★ *Elderberries*: Serve with cheeses
★ *Elderflowers*: Add to ice cream or milky puddings
★ *Lavender*: Goes with all kinds of meats, is especially good with potatoes, and try it with seafood too
★ *Mango*: With or without coriander and chillies, for your own addition to curry
★ *Mint*: A frequent addition to lamb and excellent with cheese pâté or spreads
★ *Rose petals*: For light dishes such as seafood, fish and chicken, or salads
★ *Rosemary*: Tastes great with lamb or apple dishes
★ *Rowan berries*: To go with all meats and strong cheeses
★ *Saffron*: Just a little makes a wonderful golden jelly to go with all kinds of rice dishes, ices and cakes
★ *Thyme*: Really good with pork or chicken dishes

You can mix and match these and add any others your heart, or stomach, can think of. You can also add other fruit such as plums, damsons, peaches or gooseberries to vary the base flavour of your jelly. As it is the preparation of the apples and the sterilizing of the jars which is the boring part of this recipe, I find it best to make a large batch of the mixture and subdivide it to make several flavours at the same time.

As well as being kept for your own use, herb vinegars, oils and jellies make excellent presents, especially if you can find attractive jars to package them in. Have a look at Chapter 11, 'Herb Sachets and Gifts', for other gift ideas.

Brews and Teas

'By seed and root, by stem and bud…'

 Teas can be made with the leaves, roots, stems, flowers and fruit of a great many herbs and plants. The art of steeping dried or fresh herbs in hot water goes back many thousands of years. Forget about most of the nasty powdery stuff you get in today's tea bags – it has its uses, but when it comes to drinking it really is second rate compared with the real thing. If you doubt this, then find a good-quality store which sells loose tea by weight rather than in packets and try it. This is especially true for most of the herbal teas which are on sale; being manufactured so as to have a long shelf life, they tend to need a lot of steeping, which also brings some of the bitter flavours to the fore. These teas almost always need large quantities of sugar or honey to make them palatable! If you prepare your own brews from basic ingredients you will find this gives a completely different flavour, not to mention actually promoting their health-giving or Magical properties. I would only recommend manufactured teas when you are seeking remedies for babies or young children, as they are designed to be tolerated by the young and palatable to them.

When making tea or any other herbal infusion there are certain ways of making the most of your preparation:

★ Always use china or glass and never metal or plastic, as many herbs will react with these to taint the flavour. Always use clean utensils. It used to be said that you should never really clean a teapot as this would change the taste of the tea. Too right it does – it allows you to revisit the old tired tannins and other extracts which remain on the crockery. Not a good thing!

★ Try to ensure that your kettle is clean, especially if your water supply is very chalky or has a lot of chemicals in it. Only fill your kettle with as much water as you will need – this conserves both water and electricity – and always boil freshly-drawn water, don't reboil it.

★ If you can, try to make your teas with filtered or spring water. Where you are certain there is little air pollution, rain water is ideal. For Magical brews the best results are gained by collecting rain water and exposing it, in a clear jar, to the light of the Full Moon.

★ Make your tea just before you intend to drink it and strain it as soon as the herbs have had the right amount of time to soak, even if you do intend to have a second cup. The longer the herbs remain in the water, the more any bitter taste will emerge. If you make up tea blends in advance, keep them in an airtight container in a dark and cool place, and discard unused combinations after a couple of months. No infusion should need to stand for more than 12 minutes. If it is not strong enough after that, make a note to add more of the herb next time.

★ Chilled teas will need to be covered in the refrigerator, otherwise they may take up other flavours or release their own to contaminate other foods (especially milk).

Most herb teas are not intended to be drunk more than three times a day. You can have too much of a good thing! In an ideal world the rest of your daily fluid intake would be made up of water. Herb teas are also intended to be drunk warm, not boiling, and sipped slowly, if you have a great thirst, then drink a glass of water whilst waiting for your tea to cool.

Where possible, take your time over preparing and drinking your tea, as you will find it enhances the flavour as well as the effects. Remember to inhale the aromas too. Take a tip from the Japanese, who are famous for their tea rituals: take your time.

The following blends are for one person and are intended to have half a pint of boiling water poured over them. Unless it says otherwise, allow the infusion to stand for 10 minutes before straining and do not stir, as this bruises the plants. Obviously, you can adjust the amount of water or standing time to your own taste. If you prefer your tea sweet, add a little honey, not sugar, to the strained infusion.

Magical Working Tea

Have a glass of this tea an hour before undertaking ritual or any Magical work. It helps in the preparation of both mind and body.

2 tsp rosemary leaves
1 tsp lavender flowers
grated peel of 1 orange

Divination Tea

Drink this tea an hour before undertaking any form or divination. If you wish, you can continue sipping it throughout the divination process.

3 tsp rose petals
1 tsp jasmine flowers
2 crushed bay leaves
1 pinch nutmeg
1 pinch cinnamon

Reading tealeaves is one of the older forms of divination (*see* Tealeaf Reading below). You do not need to use this recipe to perform a reading; any tea will do.

Clear Thoughts Tea

This is not only useful for study but also for whenever you want to drive out negativity and get on with life.

1 tsp rosemary
1 tsp lemon balm
1/2 tsp basil
grated peel of 1/2 a lemon
equal amount of grated grapefruit peel

Body Cleansing

This tea is for clear skin, to promote the immune system and to help remove toxins from the bloodstream.

3 tsp chopped young nettle leaves
1 tsp parsley
1/2 tsp lavender flowers
juice of 1/2 a lemon

Digestive Tea

This tea is an all-round aid to digestion,

2 tsp camomile flowers
1 tsp peppermint leaves
1 tsp lightly bruised fennel seeds

Healing Tea

Drink this to promote healing or before performing any healing Magic.

1 tsp rosemary
1 tsp rosehips (*or a couple of tsps of rosehip syrup*)
¹/₂ tsp sage
¹/₂ tsp thyme

Sleep and Dream Tea 1

This tea not only promotes a good night's sleep but also brings pleasant dreams. Valerian is not to everyone's taste, but if you do find you like it then this really is the best version to try, otherwise see the next recipe.

3 tsp rose petals
¹/₂ tsp valerian root or 1 tsp valerian leaves
a few lavender flowers

Sleep and Dream Tea 2

A less powerful version of the above.

3 tsp rose petals
1 tsp camomile flowers
¹/₂ tsp basil

Summer Tea

This tea is refreshing on any warm day or after exertion in the garden. It is equally pleasant hot or cold.

2 tsp hibiscus flowers
grated peel of 1/2 a lemon (*optional*)
grated peel of 1/2 a lime (*optional*)

Winter Tea

When the chill winds blow and you feel the need for something warming, try this – it even smells of Yule!

1 tsp cinnamon
1/2 tsp nutmeg
4 whole cloves
1 crushed cardamom seed

These are just a few of the many herb teas that you can make for yourself, either from blends or from single herbs. If you want to experiment or have a particular purpose in mind, here are the properties of some common herbs.

The Physical and Magical
Properties of Common Herbs When Infused

★ *Basil*: Gastric sedative, soothes coughs, induces perspiration to reduce fever; love, exorcism, wealth, flying, protection

★ *Bay*: Stimulates appetite, digestion; protection, psychic powers, healing, purification, strength

★ *Camomile*: Digestive aid, eyewash, gargle, calming; money, sleep, purification

★ *Dandelion*: Diuretic, digestive aid, cleanses the blood; divination, wishes, connecting with spirits

★ *Elderflower*: Alleviates colds and headaches, induces sleep; protection, healing, prosperity

★ *Fennel*: Digestive and dietary aid, expectorant, reduces catarrh; protection, healing, purification

★ *Lemon balm*: Anti-spasmodic for the digestive system, stimulant for the circulatory system, counteracts tiredness and stimulates the brain; psychic powers, longevity

★ *Marjoram*: Disinfectant and antiseptic, promotes healing, induces sleep, antidepressant; love, happiness, health, money

★ *Mint*: Refreshing, digestive aid; healing, travel, exorcism, protection

★ *Nettle*: Rich in minerals and vitamins, cleanses and purifies the blood; exorcism, curse breaking, protection

★ *Parsley*: Diuretic, helpful with joint pains, acts to take up the scent of strong-smelling foods; protection, lust, fertility

★ *Raspberry leaf*: Strengthens the female reproductive system, especially helpful if drunk regularly during the last third of pregnancy; protection, love, banishing spirits

★ *Rosemary*: Stimulates the heart and circulation; cleanses and purifies, mental powers, youth

★ *Sage*: Tonic, disinfectant, alleviates coughs, colds and fevers; longevity, wisdom, wishes

★ *Thyme*: Antiseptic and disinfectant; purification, psychic powers, courage

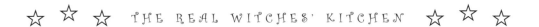

Tealeaf Reading

Tealeaf reading is one of the older forms of divination and can be practised with any kind of tea.

★ Make the tea in the usual manner but do not strain into the cups. Allow it to settle for a minute or two before drinking, so that the leaves sink to the bottom of the cup and try not to drain the cup entirely – a little fluid should be left covering the leaves.

★ Take the cup and swirl it three times so that the leaves are once again suspended in the dregs and then quickly invert the cup over a saucer. Don't bang it down or you may break the cup!

★ Then, holding the cup up to the light, examine the patterns left by the leaves on the inside of the cup.

★ There are many books which will give you explanations for the patterns you see there – a bird means travel, a ring means romance, and so on. However, as always, it is best if you can make your own interpretations of the patterns.

Like any form of divination tealeaf reading takes practice, in this case not least because of the skill involved in drinking unstrained tea. Happy drinking!

Alcoholic Brews

There are times when you want something more stimulating than a simple herb tea – when celebrating the Sabbats, feasting or holding a party, or just generally relaxing in the company of good friends. On these occasions you might want to look at stronger concoctions. Some you can buy, others you can make yourself.

Magical Fruit Wines

If you are a winemaker then you can make any of the following from first principles. If, however, you prefer a quicker method, take a cupful of the juice of any of the following and add to a bottle of good-quality white wine, either still or sparkling. Some types of fruit will go better with a sweet wine, but this really depends upon your taste. Chill for an hour before serving.

The Magical Properties of Fruit

★ *Apple*: Love, healing, immortality

★ *Cherry*: Romantic love, divination

★ *Elderberry*: Sleep, divination

★ *Elderflower*: This is not a fruit but elderflower wine is comparatively easy to find; protection, prosperity

★ *Grape*: Of course wine itself is made of grapes so you do not need to add any more to use it for fertility, garden Magic, mental powers and money

★ *Orange*: Love, luck, money, solar energy

★ *Peach*: Love, exorcism, fertility, longevity

★ *Pear*: Physical love

★ *Plum*: Healing, protection

★ *Raspberry*: Protection, love, safe childbirth (of course pregnant women should only drink in moderation, if at all, but that doesn't stop friends from wishing them well!)

★ *Rhubarb*: Fidelity, protection of the home

★ *Strawberry*: Love and luck

★ *Vanilla*: Whilst not a fruit as such, you can always add a few drops of the essence of vanilla to increase mental powers and restore energy

Stronger Brews

Those of you who like a stronger tipple can follow the lead of the Russians, who infuse their herbal remedies in vodka.

The general process is the same whether you are adding herbs, fruit (usually the peel), spices or other additives. Take a bottle of good-quality vodka (cheap vodka will taste oily) at room temperature, add your chosen flavouring and replace the cap carefully. Leave to stand at room temperature for 12 to 24 hours, tasting to see if the flavour is strong enough. Strain, then freeze for at least 6 hours before serving. You can leave the herbs, etc., in the bottle, which looks far more effective, but do be aware that even in the freezer the flavour will continue to develop.

Try the following:

★ *Basil*: 4 to 5 sprigs. Drink to promote friendship and harmony.

★ *Blackcurrant*: 2 tablespoons of the buds whilst they are still sticky. Drink as a tonic or to drive out negative influences.

★ *Cardamom*: 6 lightly crushed cardamoms. For love, romance and as an aphrodisiac.

★ *Coffee*: 12 coffee beans. You can add 6 tbsps of sugar if you fancy a liqueur flavour. Drink as a stimulant and to aid the digestion.

★ *Coriander*: 2 tsps of crushed coriander. To warm and relax, and for love and lust.

★ *Dill and garlic*: 3 sprigs of dill and 2 halved garlic cloves. This is an uplifting drink which raises the spirits and is used for protection, love, lust and money.

★ *Fennel*: 2 tsps lightly crushed seeds or the tops from 4 plants. Drink for purification, protection and healing. It is also said that eating fennel helps to avoid the attentions of insects.

★ *Lemon*: The sliced peel of a large lemon (ensure there is no pith present). This zingy drink inspires conversation and is said to bring about strong bonds of friendship as well as longevity.

★ *Mint*: 6 whole mint leaves. To aid the digestion, especially after a heavy meal, also to promote wealth and prosperity.

★ *Hot pepper*: 1 small hot (not chilli) pepper, lightly scored all over. Drink to fidelity, enduring relationships or to exorcise negative energies. It is also excellent for warding off colds and 'flu.

★ *Saffron*: Take 1/4 tsp saffron, add to 1 tsp hot water, crush thoroughly and add the paste to your vodka. Drink this golden liquid for laughter, joy, prosperity and to enhance psychic powers.

★ *Tarragon*: 3 to 4 sprigs of fresh tarragon. Drink to wisdom, fertility and divination.

Russians drink their vodka neat from very small glasses, usually with a long feast of small pieces of light foods, but be aware that whilst a little will work wonders, a lot may well have the opposite effect once the alcohol gets to your brain, not to mention the morning after!

There is no limit to the varieties of tea, wine, vodka or indeed any other drink you care to make, other than your own imagination. You can also experiment with fruit beers or other alcoholic beverages. Just remember that a good-quality base, whether vodka or water, will be the main influence on the flavour and efficacy of your finished product, so it really is worth spending that little extra, even if it means consuming less.

Looking Good, Feeling Fine

'I who am the beauty of the green earth...'

According to my grandmother's generation the secret to looking good is clean skin and hair and a friendly smile, and you know, she wasn't far wrong. Contrary to what you read and see in the media we are not all intended to look the same and we are not all attracted to the same kinds of looks. You only have to look around at couples and relationships in the real world to realize that what is considered attractive varies considerably. However, some things are generally considered unattractive, and looking and smelling unwashed comes very high on this list for almost everyone. Also on the list, again for almost everyone, are people who seem unfriendly, self-absorbed or miserable, so practise smiling! This is not just curling your mouth up at the corners, but a genuine friendly smile that reaches your eyes.

Making Friends and Influencing People

If you really want to charm someone, be it in the context of a relationship, an interview or just taking faulty goods back to the shop, then you need to learn to focus on them. Don't just act interested in them, actually *be* interested in them. Ask questions to get them to talk about themselves. Pay attention to what they are saying and ask questions to draw them out. Don't fill the conversation with your own personal thoughts, feelings or experiences unless they ask questions of you, and try to make sure that your conversation is a two-way process, not a monologue.

Look (not stare) at the person you are talking to – don't let your eyes slide around the room as though seeking a more interesting 'target'. If possible, eliminate outside distractions. Try to position yourself so that you are not looking past someone at an interesting view or room full of people. At home, always turn off the television if you're planning a serious chat. If you smile nicely and make someone the focus of your attention, you'll be surprised at just how well they respond.

Another 'truth' from my grandmother's day is 'If you can't say something good about someone, then don't say anything at all.' Always resist the temptation to run down others or to make fun of them. This does not just apply to the person you are talking to, but to anyone at all. You're not expected to actually like the whole universe, but you will seem a much nicer person if you're not seen to be negative about other people.

Of course, whilst being a nice, clean and interested person will help you make and keep friends, we all, at least occasionally, feel that our appearance needs a bit of help. In previous chapters we've looked at ways of using plants and herbs to solve problems such as illness or stress, which may affect the way we look. Here I'm going to look at some of the ways in which you can give your appearance a head start.

Eating to Live, Not Living to Eat

I'm afraid that the basis for looking good has to be a healthy diet. I say 'afraid' because you will probably have been bombarded by advice on healthy eating since you were young and so far all it has done is introduce you to a list of foods you should eat but either don't like or find hideously complicated to prepare and a second list of foods which you love but which are 'forbidden'. However, it needn't be like that – whilst you probably will have to exercise some restraint, you shouldn't have to give up everything you love in order to eat healthily.

The secrets to a healthy diet are balance and variety. Be very wary of food fashions and also of food scares, many of which have more to do with media overkill than with any real dangers in our food. For example, contrary to what you see and hear, we do need some fat in our diet (not a lot, but some) and the only person with no cholesterol is a corpse!

You can also take a long hard look at some of the things that might have been true for your parents' generation but are far less applicable in an age when there is a greater variety of foods available. By this I mean comments like 'You must eat cabbage or liver to get iron into your diet' – these days we can get it in our breakfast cereal or find it added to our milk, not to mention in a whole range of more 'interesting' vegetables. Also, there are more interesting ways of cooking nowadays. Cabbage is awful if it has been boiled to death and is served as a sludge, but cabbage leaves stuffed with cheese, tomatoes and chilli and then steamed or roasted make a very appetizing dish. And you don't have to be a brilliant cook to make the most of food – very few of us are unable to get to a store which sells a variety of interesting ready-meals.

Another myth to be wary of is the one that says a balanced diet is one where every meal is precisely engineered to contain a complete balance in every aspect. Instead, think of a balanced diet as one which evens itself out over the week, or even two weeks. This way what you eat does not take control of your life but allows you to live it more fully.

So, what constitutes a healthy balanced diet? I'm going to talk from the perspective of an omnivore with no dietary restrictions imposed by health or choice. Those of you who are vegetarian or vegan should already be able to calculate the adjustments you need to make. Those of you with special dietary needs or some form of illness or allergy should consult your doctor before making any dietary changes.

I'm also going to talk about feeding yourself in the broadest sense – not just with food and drink, but also with mental and emotional 'nutrition'.

Elemental Nutrition

As I said earlier, as Witches we believe that the elements of Air, Fire, Water, Earth and Spirit are all a part of us and represent our thoughts, passions, emotions, bodies and inner selves. In order to achieve personal growth we must work towards balance in the elements. This means setting aside parts of our lives to attend to our needs not just in terms of food but also in terms of feeding the self. In an ideal world we would be able to devote equal amounts of our lives to tending each of the elements in ways we enjoy. In the real world we often have to make compromises, but more of this later. For now, let's look at each element in turn.

Air – our Thoughts

Interesting mental stimulation is essential to a well-balanced life. Recent studies have indicated that an active mental life may reduce the chances of developing senile dementia. Alternatively, ask any parent of a baby or pre-schooler, whose life revolves around feeds, nappies, children's TV and saying 'no', just how much they crave interesting adult company and the opportunity to talk about anything not connected to child-raising. As a species we actually need to think.

Unfortunately for most of us this need is not satisfied in our daily lives. We may be at home caring for the young (which frequently includes periods of mind-numbing repetition and frustration), we may work at a repetitive and boring job, we may find that the stress of life, whilst challenging, is not stimulating in a beneficial way. So we need to set aside time on a regular basis to feed the mind.

This does not mean that you have to take up a foreign language or chess or complete the cryptic crossword in record time. What you do need to do is find something that interests you, that engages your brain and encourages you to think. It could be as simple as reading a magazine about an interest or hobby or watching non-fiction TV. (Contrary to what is often said, the TV need not be the enemy of thought, as long as you are not slumped in front of it mindlessly watching the moving wallpaper!) It could be something practical, making things, experimenting with new recipes or redesigning your interior décor. It could also be a social activity, meeting friends to discuss your lives or the world around you. In short, it can be anything which requires you to think.

Fire – our Passions

Passion does not just refer to sexual passion, it relates to your enthusiasms, to anything which makes your heart beat just a little bit faster. We are accustomed to playing down our feelings, particularly in the UK, to the extent that it is seen to be clever to 'play it cool'. Unfortunately this means that we are constantly controlling our feelings and enthusiasms and rather than being able to harness this energy, we suppress it, and in doing so lose something of ourselves.

Learning to feed your passion is not easy if you have been in the habit of suppressing it, but look around your world and see if you can identify something that fires your enthusiasm. It could be a new project, something you have always wanted to do but have always put off because it was impractical, expensive, time-consuming, any one of a hundred 'good' reasons for not doing something you really want to do. Alternatively, it might be working for or helping others. Perhaps it is learning a new skill or improving an old one. But find something which gets you enthusiastic and involved and then make the time to do it at the very least once a week.

Once you start feeding your passion in one area you will almost certainly find that you can unlock your passion for other things. And being able to demonstrate enthusiasm is also attractive and will draw others to you.

Water – our Emotions

We keep our emotions under control in much the same way as we do our passions. It isn't 'seemly' to laugh, cry or show your feelings openly. So we lock them up and through lack of use they can become atrophied and we no longer even understand the difference between appropriate and inappropriate ways of relieving them. We can become so accustomed to not hurting other people's feelings by telling them when they have hurt ours, for example, that we are in danger of letting the world use us as a doormat. We may no longer see that it is nonsensical to be crying into the pillow late at night rather than simply saying 'That really upset me' to the person who has hurt us.

Many people are frightened of letting their feelings out. Who knows what might happen? Also, you cannot just undergo a personality change overnight – those around you almost certainly won't understand, for a start. However, it is possible to start slowly. I recently heard the tale of someone who came from a very undemonstrative family where parents and grown-up children never hugged or said 'I love you'. This person loved their parents and wanted, needed, to show that affection, so they decided to 'break the ice' so to speak. One day at the end of a phone call home they said, 'I love you, Dad.' There was a long pause and the response 'You too' came back. Determined not to let things return to the way they were, this person continued and after a few months of calls and visits their parents became responsive to the extent that hugs and 'I love you' became part of family currency. I tell you this to let you know that not only can things be changed by persever-ance, but that you just might find the changes are welcomed by those around you. However, do remember to start the process gently.

Of course love is not the only emotion. Many of us also need to relearn how to be in touch with our other emotions – even to relearn the difference between loneliness and boredom or to recognize the need for some time alone. You might be surprised at how many of us try to feed our emotional needs through our mouths – eating chocolate when we really need a hug, turning to 'comfort' food when we need to talk to a friend, having a drink or cigarette when feeling justifiable anger or seeking reassurance because our confidence is low. Perhaps this isn't so surprising when you realize that almost every child gets its first easily understood praise when it makes the change to solid foods and gets subsequent reinforcement every time a plate is cleared at mealtime.

To become more in tune with your emotions, start with the easy ones. Seek out humour – in books or films or on TV – and learn to laugh out loud. Then watch a movie or read a book which is likely to make you weepy and instead of chewing a hole in the inside of your mouth, let the tears come. After any awkward or difficult situation, take time to ask your-self how you feel about it and why. At the end of the day take time to review how you feel about things in general.

For some people, one of the easiest ways to get in tune with feelings is to keep a diary. Writing down what happened in your day and how you felt about it often allows you to be more open with yourself. When I was pregnant and all my emotions were confused by hormones, medical care and more varying advice than you could shake a stick at, I kept a detailed diary of everything I felt. It didn't make the problems and worries go away, but it did help me put them into perspective. It allowed me to differentiate between justifiable anger and the sort of anger caused by worry and insecurity. And now, reading it from the perspective of a few years of parenthood, it quite often gives me an opportunity to have a good laugh at myself! However, if you are keeping a diary of your emotions, do make sure that you are the only person likely to see it. Don't put your trust in other people's self-control, as for some the sight of a diary is a temptation beyond all other, and if you once feel that your privacy has been breached you will be unlikely to really trust yourself to paper in quite the same way and hence will lose the benefit.

Earth – Our Physical Self

Our body's needs are at once simple and complex. The basic needs have been defined as food, shelter and warmth. However, being able to present our best possible self to the outside world depends upon a number of factors:

Sleep

This really is essential. When you do not have enough sleep your skin becomes dull and loses its elasticity. Your eyes are tired and may even have dark shadows under them. Your shoulders curl inwards, producing a slumped posture, and your ability to concentrate and enjoy life is reduced. It is no good trying to do your sleeping on a weekly basis – you really should get the right amount of sleep daily. You can get away with the odd short night, but it needs to be paid back as quickly as possible.

Exercise

It is true that the fitter you are, the better you will look. Regular exercise reduces excess fat, improves the circulation of the blood, increases resistance to illness and produces chemicals in the brain which, amongst other benefits, make us feel good. A few lucky people find a sport or activity that they enjoy and for which they have enough time on a regular basis. For the rest of us exercise is something that must fit into our daily lives. So, use the stairs, not the lift, and walk instead of taking the car. If you make the extra time to go for a daily walk, you can use this to get some daily peace and quiet as well. For those practising the Craft this is pretty much essential anyway, as this is when you can observe the changes in the season and the natural cycle of the Wheel of the Year.

Warmth

Reduce extremes of temperature. Going from very hot to very cold is especially bad for the skin, hair and nails. As you can do little about the outside temperatures, try to avoid over-heating your home. If you can walk around your house in just a T-shirt in winter, your heating is almost certainly too high. Your body reacts to cold by reducing the amount of blood going to the extremities, reserving it for the vital organs in your core. As a result your skin, especially on your arms, hands, legs and feet, is deprived of some nutrients, and nature being nature, it is the ones relating to your looks which go first! The best ways around this are to allow your body to acclimatize to winter gently. Unless you have a medical problem, let the temperature in your house drop to a point where you need a thick jumper and heavy socks to feel warm enough. When you go out in the cold or wet, cover up and use a suitable cream on your exposed skin.

Water

Your body needs water, lots of water. Tea, coffee and other drinks containing caffeine do not really count, nor do fizzy drinks and strong squashes. All these have the effect of driving water out of the tissues, even as they fill the stomach and bladder. Drink water, neat! The average person should drink around 6 to 8 pints of liquid per day, of which half should be plain water. Water flushes out the system, helping the liver to remove toxins from the tissues and blood. It plumps out the tissues from within, reducing signs of ageing such as wrinkles, it enables the skin to retain its elasticity. It is also cheap (if not free) and readily available to most people. If water from your tap (faucet) tastes really foul (and mine does), invest in a water filter and keep your filtered water in the fridge. Alternatively, look for an inexpensive bottled water without too many mineral ingredients. Generally speaking, the very cheap water sold in huge bottles is better than the better-known branded kind.

Grooming

Just like an expensive racehorse, we actually need regular grooming. Brushing your hair gently but thoroughly from root to tip with 100 strokes a day is a very old-fashioned approach, but it really does work. Brushing removes old dead hairs, smooths the surface of your hair to help it shine and spreads your natural oils the length of the hair to make it more manageable. Try to reduce chemical treatments for your hair – a little goes a long way. If you are using a can of hairspray (or similar) a week to keep your hair in place, then you need a new haircut. Try not to wash your hair too often either, as this removes the natural oils and encourages the hair to produce more oils of its own, thus starting a vicious cycle, until you feel that you need to wash it twice a day just to keep it reasonable.

Washing

Your skin also needs attention, and the best is washing. Avoid harsh soaps and lotions, as these all contain detergent in one way or another. In fact warm (not hot) water and a sponge or flannel (wash cloth) will be sufficient for your face most of the time. For the rest of your body, find a soap without too much perfume or make your own with natural scents (see Chapter 3, 'Soaps and Bathing Preparations'). The scents put into our cosmetics are usually chemical, not natural, with the result that oils, usually lanolin, have to be added to redress the balance.

If you are concerned about body odour, first look at your diet to see if the cause lies there. Some of us actually excrete the scents of what we eat through our skin. I'm lucky, for me it happens with strawberries. Otherwise try to find a gentle deodorant or anti-perspirant and remember that it is washing that removes the smell, sprays and roll-ons simply delay its reoccurrence or mask it. There really is nothing worse than someone who smells of body odour with a heavy overlay of cheap scent.

Protection

Before civilization became industrialized, the rain and wind were natural. Now they contain all kinds of chemicals and it is a good idea to protect your skin from them. You only have to look at the stonework on an old church or cathedral to see the effects of acid rain and whilst you will not be standing on one spot for generations, these chemicals will have an effect on any exposed areas of skin. To protect yourself, a simple moisturizer will normally suffice.

You also need to protect your skin from too much sun. The sun's rays hasten drying of the skin and ageing, and may cause skin cancer. However, we do have an inbuilt mechanism to help us with this: exposure to sunlight causes our skins to produce melanin, which in turn helps to protect against sunlight. So the trick here is not to be too extreme in either exposure to sunlight or in covering up.

When you are exposed to sunlight, take sensible precautions. Think back to the way your skin has reacted in the past. You will know if you are fair and liable to burn easily or whether your skin tans quickly. Do not simply slap on a high-factor sunscreen first thing in the morning and expect it to last all day. Choose a level of protection which is right for you (any pharmacist should be able to advise you) and reapply it several times during the day. Remember that those areas you have not exposed before will be more liable to burning, as they won't have a history of melanin production to draw on. Stay out of the noontime sun and spend time in the shade. If you are somewhere new, look to see what the locals do. They will have had generations of experience to draw on and will have developed sensible lifestyles for their part of the world.

Talking of travelling, if you want to avoid the attentions of the local insect population, use non-perfumed toileteries and cosmetics. I've spent time in North and South Africa this way without the need for huge amounts of insect repellent, and I get bitten easily.

Food

Now we come to the much-referred-to 'balanced diet'. Actually, we all know what a sensible diet is (if you are in any doubt, have a look at the food lists further on in this chapter), the problem is actually living up to it. For myself I find that the easiest way to tackle this is at the beginning – what you don't have access to won't tempt you, so it starts in the buying rather than the eating. It's old advice, but never, ever shop when hungry. If you do find yourself doing so, then try to eat a piece of fruit and drink a glass of water before you start buying. If you live with others who do keep tempting things around, then see if you can get all the temptations put into one place so at least you don't have to come across them when you're browsing for a meal or snack. If someone else is in charge of the buying and cooking, let them know that you are trying to change your eating habits and at least once a week see if you can take charge of the cooking. If you feel you still need extra help, then put a picture of yourself looking your worst close to the location of the tempting foods.

Spirit – our Inner Self

Our inner selves need as much care and attention as our bodies. One of the things nearly everyone fails to do is to nurture the spirit. This does not necessarily mean spending hours on your knees in prayer and contemplation or perfecting the art of meditation so that you are transported to another world by the sound 'Om'. Although some people do find that this meets their spiritual needs, others are more likely to find spiritual peace tending the garden or simply having a long scented bath by candlelight.

The key to feeding the spirit inside lies in having just a little personal time on a regular basis to do something which actually makes you feel good about yourself. Taking time just for yourself may seem very selfish, but it really is a basic human need and allows you to re-enter life's fray with just a bit more tranquillity.

Probably the most difficult part of this lies in remembering to take this time and getting those around you to respect it. For some strange reason, given that we all live hectic and noisy lives, very few people really understand the idea that someone might choose to spend a few quiet minutes on their own. If you tell someone that you want time to think, you will arouse their curiosity and possibly concern. Murphy's law (the one that says anything that can go wrong will) also says that if you want to contemplate whilst actually doing something, you will get a herd of helpers who all wish to talk incessantly! I don't often recommend outright lying, but this is one occasion when you might find that it's the only way to secure 20 minutes or so of peace and quiet. Probably the most effective 'story' you can give your near and dear is to tell them that you have taken up meditation (actually not all that far from the truth anyway) and need to practise regularly. Similarly, you can tell them that you are learning to meditate whilst gardening or going for a meditative walk. As just about everyone is aware that meditation needs peace and quiet and is not what you might call a spectator sport, you should be able to take yourself off without arousing a lot of curiosity.

The Balanced Whole

Every task, no matter how mundane, can and should contain references to all the elements. Even something as tedious as doing the ironing should start with thought (air): What am I going to do, where and how? Can I make it more interesting, perhaps by listening to the radio? It will involve passion (fire), even if only as an enthusiasm to get the job over and done with. Emotion (water) is reflected by the thoughts that can be generated by each garment – the last time you wore it, the next time you hope to. Your body (earth) is doing the task and how you hold yourself and flex your muscles is a form of exercise. Your spirit will be there (if perhaps a little unwillingly!) and if you are performing a repetitive task, you can allow your mind to drift a little to contemplate other, more pleasurable activities.

In the Craft we often deal with life's less pleasant chores by dedicating them to the God or to the Goddess. In this way the work becomes almost a form of sacrifice (in terms of the effort put in) as well as an opportunity to focus on an aspect of the Divine. Quite often this will pay a dividend, as work dedicated in this way seems to be easier and completed more quickly than work just undertaken as a chore.

Achieving your Best Weight

Weight is a big concern for many people, but while as a Witch I believe that we should each seek to be the best self we can, I do not subscribe to the belief that beauty lies in being unnaturally thin. The Goddess has decided that we all come in different shapes and sizes and it is no more reasonable to seek to alter our natural shape than it is to seek to alter our height or the number of fingers we have. For example, if you are naturally pear-shaped you will never have skinny hips. Also remember that your overall shape is likely to change as you get older – it is supposed to. Nature did not intend us all to look pre-pubescent at 30 or 40.

However, there are simple ways of improving your shape and one is to improve your posture. Sitting or standing in a slumped position will make you look and feel old, tired and fat. Use a full-length mirror to help you to stand up straight, take your hands out of your pockets, put your shoulders back and face the world with pride.

Another way to improve your shape is to tone up through exercise. However, do exercise in a sensible way. Don't embark on some strenuous regime which is incompatible with your life, as you won't be able to keep it up. Ignore the statement 'No pain, no gain' – if exercise hurts either you're doing it wrong or you're doing the wrong exercise.

In the veterinary world there is a very simple rule of thumb to determine whether a pet is overweight or not: if you can see the ribs at all it's too thin (for humans that would be standing naked in front of the mirror); if you can't feel the ribs with a bit of pressure from your fingers, it's too fat.

For those of you who still doubt that being thin is unattractive, think on this: a very famous fashion model, the kind who does a lot of swimsuit work, recently took time out of her career to live a 'country life'. In doing so she put on about 28 lb. She was reported in the UK press as saying she prefers her new weight and is far happier. She also said that during her very skinny years she was always tired, inclined to be shrewish, which meant that she made fewer friends, and was really quite self-obsessed when it came to food. Eating, or rather not eating, ruled her life. Oh, and by the way, she's still modelling swimwear because looking healthy and happy is so attractive.

The Witch's Diet

As I am frequently asked for advice on diet and on losing weight, I tend to give out the following 'diet sheet'. It has been described as 'the Witch's diet'; in reality it is simply a way of dividing common food groups into a sensible set of categories.

Unlimited

You can eat as much of these as you like:

★ fresh fruit and vegetables (not avocados)
★ frozen and tinned fruit and vegetables, so long as they are preserved without sugar or syrup

Sometimes

You can eat these once a day and if seeking to reduce weight you need to make it a small portion (try assigning yourself a smaller dish or bowl):

★ fresh fruit juice, without added sugar
★ milk – if trying to reduce weight make it semi-skimmed (2% milk)
★ bread
★ butter or low-fat spreads, up to 1 oz a day
★ cheese, up to 1 oz a day
★ egg, one per day
★ yeast extract spread or similar
★ lean meat or poultry, up to 4 oz per day
★ fish, non-oily if dieting
★ cereal
★ rice
★ pasta
★ pulses and lentils

Rarely

These are the treats you give yourself, ideally no more than twice a week and if seeking to reduce weight once a week or less:

★ squashes, fizzy drinks
★ sugar
★ nuts, crisps (potato chips), etc.
★ sweets, chocolates
★ cakes, biscuits
★ jams, jellies, spreads (except yeast extract spreads or similar)
★ takeaways
★ alcohol (If you really value the condition of your hair, skin and general health try not to drink alcohol. If, however, like most of us you do enjoy a drink, make sure that you drink extra water before, during and after to try to compensate.)

In addition:

★ Drink 6 to 8 pints of water a day.
★ Give up salt and use herbs instead.
★ Reduce your consumption of tea, coffee and other drinks containing caffeine.
★ Take some gentle exercise twice a day.
★ Give eating its own space – that is, try not to combine eating with any other activity such as reading or watching TV and never 'graze' (i.e. eat whilst moving around).
★ Eat at least three meals a day. Eating little and often allows your stomach to shrink (hence requiring less filling) and keeps your blood sugar levels up. If you miss or skip meals your body will assume that there is a food shortage and move into 'famine' mode where it stores as fat every calorie of food that is not immediately needed. If your body feels that food is plentiful, you will excrete more of the excess that is not needed for a healthy diet.
★ Find a healthy snackfood that you enjoy, for example apples or raw carrots, and make sure that there is always some in the house, because no matter how determined you are to eat healthy regular meals and how great your self-control, there will always be the occasion when you just need a little something to nibble.
★ If seeking to lose weight, use a smaller dish or bowl to eat from.

★ When eating pre-prepared foods, ready meals and the like, read the labels. You can easily tell whether something is all sugar, salt and chemicals or whether it contains a reasonable amount of nutrition.

Now, as with any 'diet', you can cheat. Just remember, though, you are only cheating yourself.

By the way, for those of you who now have me pegged as something of a 'health fiend', I am not vegetarian and I do enjoy chocolate and a drink. It's just that I am aware of how what I eat and drink can affect me.

Gilding the Lily

OK, so now we are eating sensibly, getting enough exercise and rest, and finding the time and space to tend to the less physical side of our nature. What else can we do to improve the way we look? Previously I cautioned against using too many chemical treatments on the skin and hair, but there are more natural treatments that you can prepare at home.

Hair

Remember not to wash your hair every day, or even every other day. Unless you have a very dirty or smelly job, it does not need it and you are simply washing out all the natural oils and encouraging the scalp to produce more, resulting in greasy roots and dry ends.

Try diluting your shampoo with water just before use – it will lather more easily, rinse out more thoroughly and save you money, as it will go further. Always rinse your hair very thoroughly. I know it feels as though you are washing out all the 'nutrients' that your hair products promised, but a build-up of those same products is the fastest route to dull life-less hair.

Get a good-quality hairbrush (preferably natural bristle) and brush your hair thoroughly and regularly, several times a day. Keep your hairbrush clean by washing it at least once a week.

Try to include the following in your diet on a regular basis; onions, watercress, broccoli, radish, garlic, seaweed, nettles (take young fresh nettle tops, cook them like spinach and serve with butter and nutmeg). Also make sure you have plenty of B vitamins, yeast extract and wholemeal (wholewheat) bread or take a dietary supplement such as Brewer's yeast (this is not the same as yeast used in brewing!)

Enhance Colour and Shine

Whether your hair colour is natural or not, you can enhance it by using rosemary if you are a brunette or redhead and camomile if you are blonde. Simply take a small handful of the herb, dried or fresh, pour a pint of boiling water over it and allow it to cool. Strain it and use as a final rinse. Do not rinse off.

Actually blondes have it easier here because camomile tea bags can be used (it takes three or four for the average head of hair), saving the small effort of making sure you strain all the bits out before use.

Conditioning Treatment

To condition dry or overtreated hair, warm a couple of teaspoons of good-quality oil, such as almond or peach nut, stroke it through your hair, concentrating on the ends and any-where else which feels particularly in need, and leave it on for about 10 minutes before washing off with a mild shampoo. Olive oil can also be used, so long as you really make sure it is all washed out. You can also add a couple of drops of essential oil to your warm oil treatment.

Another old-fashioned remedy is to beat the yolks of one or two eggs, massage them into your hair and leave them on for 10 minutes. They must be rinsed out with cool water, though, otherwise they will cook on your head and be near impossible to remove!

Split Ends

Contrary to the earnest wishes of the advertisers, you cannot actually repair split ends – have them cut off instead. To prevent them coming back too soon, try not to overheat or overtreat your hair. However, you can temporarily improve the appearance of your hair by using one of the conditioning treatments above.

Greasy Hair

Add the juice of a lemon and a teaspoon of vinegar to ½ pint of warm water, rinse the hair, wait 10 minutes then rinse again with cool water.

Dandruff

First, check that you do actually have dandruff. One of the most common causes of a flaky scalp is not rinsing, shampoo, conditioner or other hair treatments out properly. To really thoroughly cleanse the hair and scalp, add a couple of drops of tea tree oil to your shampoo.

The second thing to check for is an allergy to a new product, especially if you have just changed your brand of washing powder or fabric conditioner. Remember your head spends about eight hours in direct contact with your pillow.

Lastly, check that it's not just a dry scalp by giving yourself the warm oil treatment described above with a couple of drops of tea tree oil.

If you still have a flaky scalp, you might like to try:

★ The warm oil treatment mentioned under 'Conditioning' with a couple of drops of lavender and rosemary together with either cypress or cedarwood.

★ Adding ½ oz maidenhair fern to just under ¼ pint boiling water, simmering for 10 minutes, cooling and straining, then rubbing into the scalp two to three times a week.

168

★ One of the scalp massages mentioned below, under 'General Hair and Scalp Conditioning'.

If everything else fails you might want to consult a dermatologist, as most of the preparations available without prescription are at best short-term fixes rather than cures.

Nits or Headlice

Regrettably, being clean does not discourage these pests one bit. They are transmitted, usually among young children, from head to head by contact or by sharing a brush or comb. So always use your own grooming equipment. To deter them, do not wash the hair too often. Hair which is slightly greasy is less attractive to nits than hair which allows them a firm grip! Brush very thoroughly from scalp to ends at least twice a day and keep a close watch for any signs of eggs – small white objects clinging to individual hairs.

If you are unlucky and nits turn up on any family member, or you are warned that they are present at your child's school, then you need to treat the whole family immediately.

★ Take 1 fl oz of sunflower, almond or olive oil. Add 25 drops of lavender, 25 drops of rosemary, 12 drops of eucalyptus and 13 drops of geranium. Lightly warm the oil and comb through the hair very thoroughly. Wrap the head (not the face!) in a plastic bag (a carrier with one side cut works wonderfully) and leave for a couple of hours. Then comb the hair again, using a nit comb and making sure that you get all the dead (or at least stunned) nits out of the hair, before washing it thoroughly.

★ Alternatively take 3¹/₂ fl oz of base oil and add 20 drops of rosemary, 20 drops of lavender, 20 drops of basil and 20 drops of lemongrass. Use as the preceding recipe.

★ Treat every hairbrush and comb, and any other hair fixings, to a really good clean with shampoo to which you have added a couple of drops of tea tree oil. Towels, pillowcases, hats and so on should also be given a thorough wash just in case there's a stray egg or two hiding in them. Repeat the treatment weekly if you have had nits or every second week if you have simply been warned of an outbreak.

★ Tea tree oil can also be added to your regular shampoo to deter nits.
Add 20 drops to 1 fl oz of shampoo.

As I write this I have recently been given a new treatment and preventative conditioner, by Neal's Yard, London (who do mail order), which contain quassia. I can only report that thus far there has been no recurrence of the problem despite it being fairly endemic at my son's school.

General Hair and Scalp Conditioning

Hair is formed within the scalp, so many hair problems, such as thin or brittle hair and lank lifeless hair can be alleviated by action upon the scalp. Regular massaging of the scalp can produce long-term improvements. Either learn to do this for yourself or take it in turns with a friend. You are looking for a gentle massaging action which stimulates the hair follicles, not the sort of deep massage which you associate with muscular aches and pains. Also, the massage should be of the scalp, not of the hair itself, otherwise those with longer hair will find that they end up with tangles that take forever to comb out. The easiest way to tell if the massage is right is to listen to your body. If it feels good, it most probably is; if it feels uncomfortable, or even painful, then it's probably not doing you any good.

You can either massage with an oil or you can use an alcohol or acid-based rub. Either way you will need to do this just before washing with a gentle shampoo. Try one of the following:

★ *Lemon and cider vinegar*: Take a whole lemon, without the pips, reduce it in a
blender, sieve it and add to an equal amount of cider vinegar.

★ *Nettle and cider vinegar*: Chop the whole part and add to two parts water, one part
cider vinegar, bring to the boil and simmer for 30 minutes, strain and cool.

★ *Vodka and essential oil*: For dry hair, add a couple of drops of lavender or
rosemary to 1 tablespoon of vodka. For greasy hair, use bergamot or geranium.
Remember the precautions mentioned earlier on the use of essential oils.

★ *Rosemary in almond oil*: Add a handful of the fresh herb or a tablespoonful of the dried herb to about 1 fl oz of the oil, warm through gently, then bottle and leave for a week. Store in a cool dark place. This will only keep for about a month, so use it regularly.

★ *Bay rum*: This is a very traditional rubbing lotion and was thought to be especially good for bringing life and shine as well as enhancing the colour of dark hair.

Skin

Generally speaking, the skin needs to be fed from within, so you need that healthy diet, exercise and sleep. Anything you put on the outside may help the short-term appearance but is really only going to affect the surface layer of dead and dying cells. Some products in fact do more harm than good. Avoid anything highly scented or with harsh detergents, and remember to rinse well.

Having said that, you do need to protect the skin from the ravages of pollution, weather and from extremes of temperature, so some kind of moisturizer is a good idea. Experiment to find the one which suits you best. Most large stores will allow you to try their products and some even provide sample pots to take away. Be a bit cheeky – whenever you visit someone, ask if you can try some of the product(s) they use. Try to ensure that the product you finally choose is either unscented or lightly scented so that you can use it as a base for other preparations you can make at home. You can of course make your own, but in the real world very few of us are going to have the time or the equipment to start blending lanolin (or other oils) with water in a way which doesn't separate out or go off quickly. Don't assume that expensive is best. My favourite is a fairly inexpensive unscented hand-cream which comes in economy bottles and can be purchased from almost every chemist, drugstore, supermarket or local corner shop, and it's great for using as a base for essential oil or herbal preparations.

When treating your skin, don't forget about your nails, elbows and the soles of your feet. These are all hard-working areas which need extra attention. Also remember your neck. The neck is one of the biggest tell-tale indicators of age and health, yet many people spend a fortune on looking after their face only to let the care stop at the chin line.

Dry Skin

Dry skin is often caused or exacerbated by dehydration, so make sure that you drink plenty of water and cut down on caffeine, alcohol and tobacco. Here are some other ways of avoiding dry skin:

★ Try to avoid hot dry atmospheres. If you have the heating on, place a dish of water on or near your heaters or place a damp cloth on your radiator.

★ Do not sleep in a hermetically sealed room. Leave one window open at least a fraction to allow ventilation.

★ Eat apricots, avocados, sunflower or sesame seeds and oily fish such as mackerel or herring, and copy the Mediterranean habit of eating olive oil on fresh bread.

★ Try not to use soap and if you really must make sure that it is mild and unperfumed. Baby soap is ideal.

★ Find a good, easily absorbed moisturizer and use it at least three times a day.

★ After eating an avocado, rub the inside of the skin over your face or other affected areas, leave for 10 minutes and rinse with tepid water.

★ Massage affected areas with almond oil to which you have added a couple of drops of camomile or rose oil.

★ For the face you can make a mask of oatmeal (rolled oats) and honey. Leave it on for 15–20 minutes before rinsing it off thoroughly. Don't do this if there are likely to be wasps or bees about!

Itchy Patches

These are frequently caused by dry skin, so have a look at some of the remedies above. Other causes are allergy or insect bites. In all cases use lavender oil to ease irritation and to promote healing. Lavender oil can be applied direct to most skins or you can dilute it with almond oil or your favourite moisturizer.

In the case of allergy, try to track down the allergen, otherwise the condition will certainly come back again. It may be a new product or one you have been using for some time, as allergies can sometimes arise for no obvious reason. You may have changed your body chemistry, perhaps through a course of antibiotics or a change of contraceptive pill. Also look at products you use on things which come into contact with your skin. Soap powder is a regular culprit!

To avoid insect bites, don't use scented products, soaps, deodorants, shampoos or lotions. Also try to reduce your sugar intake. If you are in a country where there is a high number of biting insects, burn citronella or bergamot oil in an oil burner. Do not place these oils in direct contact with your skin, as they may cause other problems such as a reaction to sunlight, although it is possible to carry a tissue with a couple of drops on in your pocket.

There is one other condition which is, thankfully, quite rare these days: ringworm. This fungal skin infection can be picked up from dogs, cats and even passed amongst children. This can usually be treated in humans with tea tree oil, diluted 10 drops to ½ fl oz of carrier oil and rubbed in and not rinsed off. If this doesn't do the trick then see your doctor. It is best to take your pet to a vet, as modern systemic treatments are very swift-acting and prevent re-infection. Please, please do not have your pet put down because it has transferred ringworm to you or your family. It used to be standard practice for some authorities to recommend this, but it really is unnecessary. After all, you wouldn't apply the same logic if you contracted the condition through human contact.

Excessive Redness

Reddened skin can be caused by a number of problems; being too dry, being exposed to the cold and/or wet, too much sunlight, too much alcohol. In all these cases it is the underlying cause which needs to be addressed. Remember to protect your skin with a moisturizer and where necessary with a sunscreen.

To disguise the problem, look for green face powder. This rather unlikely-sounding product will not, if used sparingly, make you look like a Martian, but will tone down the redness. It is also helpful to increase your intake of chlorophyll by eating green vegetables such as lettuce, broccoli and spinach.

You can make an elderflower lotion by steeping the crushed flowers of several elderflower heads in a couple of teaspoons of alcohol. Leave for a week, sieve and add to a pint of water. This can be splashed on the skin after washing with tepid water, and will help to cool and soothe.

Cucumber is also excellent for cooling off red skin. Either place slices all over the affected area and leave for 10 minutes or peel and liquidize (or sieve) half a cucumber and add the juice to a little natural yoghurt and smooth on, leaving for about 10 minutes.

Greasy Skin

Oily or greasy skin is caused by overactive sebaceous glands. Most people will suffer from this condition at some time in their life, often during adolescence when the body's hormones are making many changes. To a certain extent you cannot make the problem just go away, but you can alleviate it:

★ Drink plenty of water, eat plenty of fresh fruit and vegetables, and stay away from greasy, fatty foods and sugar.

★ Do not use harsh chemicals, as by stripping away oils from the skin they simply encourage the skin to produce more. Astringent lotions have the same effect. Rather, take a gentle approach, using mild soap and tepid water to wash and a facial tonic such as rose water (available in most pharmacies) to rinse.

★ Use a very light moisturizer, adding a little cucumber juice.

★ Lemon or apple juice can also be used on greasy skin. Dab it on and leave for up to 15 minutes before washing off with cold water. Alternatively, add it to some sparkling (carbonated) mineral water and use as a facial spray, making sure it does not get into the eyes.

Spots

There are many different kinds of spots or pimples and, with the exception of hormonal acne, most will benefit from improving the circulation by massage.

★ To really stimulate the circulation, take a spoonful of semolina (farina) or couscous and add to a spoonful of half water, half almond oil, and massage using gentle circular movements with your fingertips. Do not scrub.

★ Alternatively, make an oatmeal (rolled oats) paste with a little water, apply it in a thin layer and rinse off with tepid water after 15 minutes.

★ The elderflower lotion described above is also useful. Dab it on with cotton wool (cotton balls), taking care not to transfer bacteria from one area to another.

Acne, that distressing condition which affects over half the people going through puberty, and an unfortunate few for many years afterwards, needs a rather more concerted approach. Whilst many medical practitioners believe that diet has nothing to do with healing acne, few herbal or natural healers would agree. It is very much a question of giving the body the best tools with which to cope with the hormonal revolution which is taking place and not overburdening the system with things that need to be excreted via the skin.

Again, look to fresh fruit and vegetables, preferably raw or only partially cooked. Drink plenty of water, herbal teas containing lavender, sage and camomile, and vegetable juices, such as carrot, lettuce and cucumber.

The list of things to avoid is quite daunting: red meat, oily fish, fats and fatty food, sugar and food with too many additives. I'm afraid that rules out almost all takeaways, ready-meals, snack foods and interesting drinks. Oh, and absolutely no alcohol.

Also, it is far better to eat little and often, up to six times a day if possible, as this gives the system the opportunity to work at a more steady pace.

Try to get regular exercise in the fresh air, as this keeps the whole system on its toes.

Steaming the skin will encourage pustules to erupt before they get too large and to heal more quickly afterwards. Place a towel over your head above a bowl of hot (not boiling) water containing lavender or camomile, and steam for five minutes. Rinse off with tepid water, then dab on rose water and leave to dry naturally.

Pimples can also be treated with tea tree oil on a cotton bud (check first to see if using it neat causes you a problem).

If you feel the need to use any kind of cosmetic to reduce the appearance of pimples, make sure it is unscented and apply it carefully with clean fingers to avoid transferring bacteria from one place to another.

Feet

Feet carry us around all day every day. When they're in good condition they're easy to forget, but if they have problems they're impossible to ignore and can affect every aspect of your life. So prevention is definitely better than cure.

Try to spend as much time as possible walking barefoot, even if it's only around the house. It will strengthen the joints, muscles, tendons and ligaments in your feet and allow them to relax from the confines of shoes. This is especially important for children, so set a good example! If you do this regularly you will also find that whilst you have less hard dry skin on your feet, they will toughen in a more general way and so it will become more comfortable to walk barefoot.

At least once a week try to give your feet a treat.

★ Wash them thoroughly and rub briskly at any dead skin with a pumice stone or rough cloth.

★ Use a nail brush on and around your toenails.

★ Dry them really carefully, as many foot problems are caused or exacerbated by dampness.

★ Now that they are clean and dry, if necessary cut the nails, straight across, as cutting down the sides encourages ingrown toenails.

★ Now give your feet a massage. A drop of peppermint oil in your moisturizer feels wonderful, especially on tired feet, and don't forget to massage the nails too. If the skin on your feet is very dry, use an oil such as almond instead of the moisturizer.

★ Lastly, put your feet up for 10 minutes – lying on the floor with them resting on a chair or on the bed with them raised on pillows is ideal.

This treatment can be done often and really does help tired aching feet and also those that feel hot enough to catch fire!

In fact raising the feet and legs a little above the head for a short period every day generally improves your feeling of well-being, as well as giving you 10 or so minutes of well-earned relaxation.

Another way to 'lift' tired feet is to soak them in a bowl of tepid water with a couple of tablespoons of Epsom salts for 20 minutes before drying them properly.

Athlete's foot, or any other fungal infection, will also benefit from the above, but add a couple of drops of tea tree oil to the washing water or to the massage oil. In severe cases, apply tea tree oil to clean dry feet, between the toes and around the nails, twice a day. It can be used undiluted, but do a skin test a day before to check that your skin will tolerate it.

Where the skin is cracked and split, apply petroleum jelly to the clean dry foot, cover with a clean cotton sock and wear it overnight. You can add a drop of frankincense or patchouli oil to the petroleum jelly if you wish.

Corns and bunions are generally caused by ill-fitting shoes, so you will need professional help to sort out the problem, as well as the co-operation of a good shoe-fitter for the future. However, you can ease the pain by regular massages of a good-quality oil to which several drops of lavender have been added.

Chilblains, those painfully itchy patches of inflamed skin, are caused by exposing cold feet to too much heat too quickly. Try not to toast your toes in front of the fire! If you do get chilblains, give your feet a good friction rub with lavender oil blended with a couple of drops of black pepper.

Hands

Your hands are the second most hardworking part of your skin after your feet. They are also almost continuously on show, so it makes sense to pay them some attention.

Many of the treatments described for feet can also be used on the hands, but probably the most important thing you can do for them is to make absolutely sure that whenever they come into contact with detergents and other chemicals you wash them thoroughly. It may seem strange to suggest that you wash your hands after doing the dishes, but you really don't want traces of the stuff you use to remove dried-on egg or burnt fat in contact with your skin for longer than necessary.

Another key thing is to ensure that you always dry your hands thoroughly. Many people give them a casual wipe on the towel and then wonder later why the skin dries and the nails flake. Also, use a good-quality handcream to which you've added a couple of drops of lavender oil. Don't just rub it on, take a few moments to really massage it in, paying special attention to the joints and around the nails.

For most of us our hands spend a lot of time in contact with soaps, detergents, and so on, so give your hands a special treat and wash them with oatmeal (rolled oats). Make a paste of oats and water and rub this in. Rinse it off with tepid water and then rub with dry oatmeal until no trace of water remains. It's messy, but really does improve the condition of the skin.

Another great way to treat your hands is to knead bread. It exercises the joints, improves the circulation, deep cleanses the skin (but do make sure they are scrupulously clean first) and moisturizes all in one!

Scents

People's impression of us is not only what they see. Whilst sight is, for most of us, the primary sense, we do in fact use our other senses too, if on a less conscious level. How a person sounds and smells also affects the way we feel about them. Indeed, in close relationships how a person tastes and feels to the touch becomes really important. Here I am going to talk about the sense of smell and how we can use it to our advantage.

First and foremost has to be the absence of unpleasant odours. As I said earlier, you cannot use perfumes and deodorants to cover up body odour, you have to tackle it at its source, and that usually means regular washing and attention to diet. Even the most fastidious person will smell strongly if they overindulge in alcohol, curry, garlic and other odoriferous foods. While you can alleviate this by chewing a cardamom seed at the time of your meal and can remove the immediate effect on the breath by chewing parsley after eating, you will only remove the residual odour by waiting until after the body has processed the offending food and then washing all over. Of course this is not such a problem if you are only going to be in contact with others who ate the same as you, in which case none of you will be able to detect each other's smell. For this reason a shower in the morning is more effective than one at night, as most of us eat strong-smelling foods in the evening, giving the body all night to process and excrete any odours.

Other than general body odour the next most obvious one is foot odour. The key to avoiding this is good foot care (see above) and good shoe care. It should come as no surprise that if you wear one pair of trainers all day, every day, they will soon accumulate sweat which attracts the bacteria that cause foot odour. In addition to spending some time every day barefoot, not only giving your feet a break but also allowing your shoes to recover, it is a good idea to alternate between several pairs of shoes if possible. If this is not practical, then make a point of changing your socks at least once a day, more if you are particularly active or suffer from smelly feet. Never wear trainers, or other fully enclosed footwear, without socks, as any perspiration can only be absorbed by the shoe. Remember, socks wash far more easily than shoes.

The next most sensitive zone is the mouth. There is nothing worse than bad breath, except perhaps having to tell someone they have bad breath! Here the top priority has to be good dental care. I know just how dreaded a trip to the dentist can be, but it really must be done. On top of that care for your teeth regularly, brush properly at least twice a day (preferably after every meal), use a mouthwash and floss. It really will pay dividends in the long run. If you can stand it, brush occasionally with bicarbonate of soda (sodium barcarbonate), as this also helps to reduce plaque.

If you have eaten something strong, then chewing fresh parsley will remove the smell, but remember to check you haven't any green bits left between your teeth afterwards. Don't reach for the peppermints, as peppermint oil can actually help cause cavities.

The other major factor in bad breath is the condition of your digestion. You'd be surprised how many mothers of small children can tell when their offspring need to move their bowels by smelling their breath. So pay attention to your body's needs and work on that healthy diet.

As well as making ourselves less smelly, there are ways we can utilize scent to change people's perception of us in a positive way. Foremost in this area is the use of aromatherapy oils. These oils not only smell nice but also contain airborne components which can actually alter the mood of not only the wearer but also of those around them.

Unlike commercial perfumes and scents, aromatherapy blends tend to remain the same throughout the day and are far less likely to be affected by a person's skin or body chemistry. They can be used in the bath for a subtle effect or blended with a base oil to make a perfume. When using a blend in this way it should always be applied sparingly – if you leave a trail of scent behind you then not only does it give the game away, but can also be quite unpleasant for those around you. Remember that if you can smell your own scent then it is probably too strong, as we quickly get used to anything we are wearing.

Here are some essential oil blends you might like to try:

Increased Self-Confidence

5 drops ylang ylang
5 drops sandalwood

To Appear More Attractive to Others

3 drops jasmine
3 drops neroli
3 drops ylang ylang

To Increase Focus and Concentration

5 drops rosemary
3 drops basil

Before an Interview

2 drops sandalwood
2 drops frankincense
2 drops rosemary
1 drop jasmine

To Aid Sleep

5 drops lavender
2 drops valerian

★ Note: *Valerian is very attractive to some cats, so if you have one you may need to shut it out of the bedroom or place a couple of drops on its favourite sleeping place to avoid being pestered!*

To Calm a Tense Atmosphere

5 drops frankincense
3 drops jasmine

To Reduce Symptoms of PMT

4 drops geranium
3 drops lavender
2 drops rose
1 drop bergamot

The Morning After the Night Before

3 drops rosemary
3 drops rosewood
3 drops rose
This also works in a tepid bath.

For a Romantic Evening

3 drops cardamom
2 drops rose

To Reduce Tantrums in Young Children

2 drops camomile
3 drops lavender
Place on a tissue for them to sniff or use in an oil burner.

In all cases remember the cautions on the use of aromatherapy oils mentioned in Chapter 2, 'Guidelines for Buying, Using and Storing Herbs and Plants', and if in doubt consult an aromatherapist.

Herb Sachets and Gifts

'May we meet and know and love once again…'

Herb sachets are used to fragrance the house, as wards of protection and defence, and can even be carried on the person. In addition to herbs, flowers, spices, leaves, and so on, they may also contain stones, charms or crystals, all imbued with Magical energies. Some people even create totem bags which also contain pictures of their loved ones, a lock of hair or many other things which link them to those they care about. Herb sachets make excellent gifts or ways of working Magic for others. Much of the work of the Witch is for other people and many of the other ideas in this book will not so easily survive a trip though the post!

Sachets can be made from almost any natural fabric; it does not have to be specially bought for the purpose. Whilst silk squares look very attractive, you can recycle old clothes, or cloths, or anything else you have to hand.

Make sure the fabric is thoroughly washed and if you have any doubts about its psychic cleanliness then hang it overnight in the light of the Full Moon before use. The easiest shape to use is a circle, but a square also looks quite attractive. Place your ingredients in the centre and tie up all the ends to create a bundle. To tie your sachet(s) you can use thread, cord, ribbon or even twine or string.

If giving sachets away, it is a good idea to make them reasonably discreet – not everyone wants their home to look as though a Witch lives there. Alternatively, you can make them highly decorative in their own right, perhaps by placing several sachets onto a strip of attractive ribbon which can then be hung on the wall. Remember whilst making up your sachet to keep your Magical goals clearly in mind and to imbue it with Magical power.

If you want the sachet to look decorative then you do not have to stick to single-colour fabric, but try to choose something where the right colour for your intention is fairly dominant. Alternatively, you can cover the sachet twice, once for the Magical intent and once with an overlay which is in keeping with the décor of the area it is intended for.

Here are some ideas for herb sachets.

Tranquil Home

This is a sachet to bring about peace in the home. It is an excellent one to give to anyone who has just moved house.

3 parts jasmine flowers
3 parts rose petals
3 parts rosemary
1 part lavender
1 part bay

Place in a pink cloth tied with green ribbon or cord and hang it over the main entrance to the home.

Protection

If you feel concerned about negative influences or thoughts coming your way, hang a small sachet of this in each window (you can hide them behind the curtains if you wish) and above each external door.

3 parts rosemary
2 parts fennel seed
1 part juniper
1 part dill seed
1 dried chilli pepper
1 part the outer dry skin of garlic
1 part coarse salt (*rock salt*)

Place in a red cloth tied with a black cord. If you think you know who might be harbouring negative thoughts about you, then you can also place a small mirror facing outwards in the window which most closely points in their direction. This will reflect back any negativity.

Sacred Space

If you regularly use the same part of your home for your Magical work then hang this sachet in that area to retain the Magical integrity and positive energies created whilst working. Just before starting any Magical act take the sachet down and carry it around your working space three times to release those Magical energies. Use a violet cloth tied with a silver and gold cord.

2 parts jasmine
2 parts rose petals
2 parts rosemary
1 part bay
1 part cinnamon (*either use 1 stick or 1 part powdered*)
1 part fennel
1 part coarse salt (*rock salt*)

Psychic Awareness

Use a violet or indigo cloth tied with a silver cord.

1 part bay
1 part cinnamon
1 part peppermint
1 part rosemary
1 part thyme

To promote psychic development, carry this at all times for one full lunar month and sleep with it under your pillow. To enhance the Magic, add the following if you can find them:

5 rowan berries
a piece of fallen wood from a rowan tree

Safety and Protection for the Car/Motorbike

Place the following into a violet cloth tied with a cord of the same (or similar) colour as your vehicle:

3 parts rosemary
2 parts juniper
2 parts basil

1 part fennel
1 part coarse salt (*rock salt*)
a few drops of peppermint oil

Place the sachet in the glove compartment or suspend it from the rear-view mirror.

This formula works just as well for a motorcycle – place it in one of the panniers or carry it on your person when riding.

Travel Protection

Wrap the following ingredients in a dark purple or indigo cloth tied with a white cord:

1 part basil
1 part fennel
1 part rosemary
1 part mustard seed
1 large pinch of coarse salt (*rock salt*)
1 small clear quartz crystal

Carry this on your person when undertaking any journey, especially one where you are a passenger. It is also said that to ensure a safe journey and happy return home you should place a small fig branch before your door.

Luck and Money

To increase good fortune and bring money your way, hang this sachet over the main entrance to the house and bury a coin just outside the door so that everyone entering has to pass over it. This charm does not guarantee untold wealth, but it does work to give you the opportunities to ensure that you have enough for your needs. Tie the following in a green cloth with a gold cord:

2 parts basil

2 parts mint
1 part jasmine
1 part pine kernels
1 part rice
1 whole nutmeg
1 almond
5 star anise seeds

Healing

Wrap all the ingredients in a violet cloth tied with violet ribbon and anoint the sachet with 3 drops of eucalyptus oil.

2 parts lavender
2 parts cinnamon
2 parts sandalwood
1 part rose petals
1 part ginger
1 part cayenne pepper
½ whole nutmeg

Carry the sachet on your person or hang it over the bed of anyone who is unwell. As soon as the illness is over the sachet should be destroyed (*see* Chapter 1, 'Witchcraft and Empowering your Herbal Work', on the disposing of spells).

Warding Off Colds and Flu

This recipe is very similar to the one above, but is intended for preventive use during that part of the year when such contagions are rife. Make a reasonable quantity so that you can carry a small sachet with you and hang one over your bed and one over the main entrance to the house. Place in small pieces of lavender cloth tied (or sewn) with black thread.

4 parts lavender

2 parts cinnamon

1 part sandalwood

1 part ginger

1 part cayenne pepper

4 whole cloves

1 whole nutmeg, split into pieces

(*wrap it in a towel and give it a sharp tap with a rolling pin*)

Reconsecrate the sachets by placing them overnight in the light of the Full Moon at every Full Moon until the season is over.

Focus and Study

As well as being of use for study and examinations, this sachet can also help those who have need of inspiration and concentration, especially authors! Place the ingredients in a dark blue cloth tied with violet cord and hang it in the bedroom or over the work area of anyone who is studying. A small sachet can also be made to be carried, especially during the exam period.

2 parts rosemary

2 parts basil

1 part caraway seed

1 part the dried rind (*not the pith*) of a grapefruit

Communication

2 parts rosemary
2 parts basil
1 part mace
1 whole almond

Wrap in a green cloth tied with indigo (blue-black) cord or thread. Carry with you to interviews or potentially difficult encounters.

True Love

To find your true love, carry this with you at all times.

2 parts rose petals
2 parts jasmine flowers
1 part lavender
1 part sandalwood

If you can, add a small rose quartz crystal to the mix and place the whole in pink cloth tied with silver cord.

A word of caution, though: do not assume that the first person you meet after preparing this is the right one!

'Little Fingers' Sachet

This one is less of a Magical charm and more of a practical aid if you have small children in your home, as it prevents them from shutting their fingers in doors.

Take two circles of fabric and stuff each tightly with fabric offcuts. Tie each into a tight ball on either end of a piece of string, cord or ribbon about 2 foot long. Hang this over the door at the hinge end so that it interferes with the closing of the door. Repeat for any doors you feel may provide a temptation.

If you wish, you can combine the useful aspect of these 'door stops' with the Magical influences of any of the above herb combinations.

Other Gifts

Sachets are excellent ways of passing your Magic on to someone who has requested it. They also make great gifts, as you can wish someone well at the same time as giving them a scented gift to hang in their home. Of course you do not have to stick to the format of a ball tied with cord – you can make small decorative cushions, or pillows as they are often called. Very small pillows used to be placed into clothes drawers to ensure that they smelled pleasant, as well as to ward off moths without the smell of mothballs (camphor). You can also add the herbs and so on to a doll or stuffed animal, as long as you can also be sure that small fingers will not open it and access the ingredients.

Of course almost all the suggestions in this book will make good gifts, it just depends on how far away the recipient is.

Floral Decoration

Dried flowers and herbs can do more than just sit in vases attracting dust and generally looking rather sad. If dried whole they can be wound onto wicker frames, which are available in a variety of shapes (including the pentacle) from many florists, and turned into decorations for the home. You can even make your own wicker frames if you can get hold of flexible wicker, or withies.

Alternatively, dried flowers and herbs can be arranged in a small basket or as a posy in a small vase. Many flowers and herbs also lend themselves to being pressed and can be made into pictures, bookmarks or decorations for furniture, trays, etc. Once a plant has been successfully pressed it can be varnished onto almost any surface, or even placed under transparent sticky-backed plastic, if you are certain it will not come into contact with heat. Plants can even be waxed onto the outside of candles (*see* Chapter 5, 'Candles and Incenses'). In these ways you can place your charms around the home without making the house look overly 'Witchy'!

Drying Plants

There are two main ways of drying plants. The first is to place them in a single layer in a warm dry place and let the moisture evaporate naturally. Natural drying can take anything from a couple of days to a couple of weeks, depending on the plant and where you dry it. However, many plants lose their colour and attractive appearance when dried this way.

The main alternative is to dry plants with silica gel. You will need a large tin – an old biscuit tin is good – and a quantity of silica gel crystals, which are available from most florists. Place the plants on a bed of crystals and cover them very gently, but completely, with more crystals. Make sure that you do not squash the flowers in the process – use a teaspoon to place the crystals in and around the flower heads. Wait a few days then gently shake off the crystals. Keep the gel in a dry place for future use.

Pressing Flowers

Most herbs and flowers also lend themselves to being pressed. Simply arrange your plant on a sheet of blotting paper (kitchen towel folded double will do) and place a second sheet carefully over the top. Now, taking care not to disturb the arrangement, place a number of heavy books on top. Leave for a couple of weeks before checking to see whether your material has dried out and become stiff. (If you want, you can check after a couple of days just to see if it is pressing into the shape you require and, if necessary, dispose of any 'non-starters'.)

Most plants press quite successfully, but the time it takes will vary according to the thickness of the plant and the amount of moisture it contains.

The Language of Flowers

In addition to making gifts which are composed using the Magical properties of the plants, you can also use them to communicate. In times gone by it used to be quite common to 'say it with flowers' and each flower, herb and plant had its own meaning. You could bring these attributes into your life by growing the appropriate plants in the garden or send a message to someone in a bouquet of flowers.

Many of these traditional plant meanings differ quite a lot from the medicinal or Magical actions of the plants. Here are just a few examples:

★ *Almond blossom*: Hope
★ *Apple blossom*: Preference
★ *Basil*: Good wishes
★ *Bay*: Glory
★ *Bluebell*: Constancy
★ *Camomile*: Patience
★ *Catnip*: Courage
★ *Dandelion*: Oracle
★ *Elderflower*: Compassion, consolation
★ *Eucalyptus*: Get well, take care
★ *Fennel*: Flattery
★ *Fern*: Sincerity
★ *Forget-me-not*: Fidelity, true love
★ *Hawthorn* (or May) blossom: Hope
★ *Heather*: Admiration, protection

★ *Honeysuckle*: Devotion
★ *Jasmine (yellow)*: Happiness, elegance
★ *Lavender*: Silence, peace
★ *Marjoram*: Health, happiness
★ *Mint*: Virtue
★ *Orange blossom*: Purity, loveliness
★ *Parsley*: Festivity
★ *Peppermint*: Warmth of feeling
★ *Poppy*: Consolation
★ *Rose*: The language of roses is quite
complex but, for example, white means 'I am worthy of you',
while red means love, and red and white mean unity
★ *Rosemary*: Remembrance
★ *Sage*: Esteem
★ *Thyme*: Activity
★ *Violet*: Modesty

Uses for Dried or Pressed Plants

There are many ways in which you can use dried or pressed plants. Here are some ideas.

Cover your Magical Journal or Book of Shadows

This is a book which you want to protect from prying eyes, so why not use a touch of herblore to help?

Press a selection of the following herbs and flowers and arrange them on the front of your book. Use a little clear adhesive to hold them in place and then cover with self-adhesive plastic, taking care not to let any air bubbles form on the surface.

★ Alchemilla, basil, bay, cinnamon, foxglove, lily and rosemary for protection
★ Dill for Magical charm
★ Fern, mistletoe, poppy and wolfsbane for invisibility
★ Honeysuckle, violet and yarrow for scrying
★ Vervain for enchantment

If you can find one, place a lotus flower (for mystery and truth) at the centre of your design.

If you would rather be overtly 'Witchy', use aconite, belladonna, foxglove, mistletoe, poppy, skullcap, toadflax, valerian, wormwood, yarrow, yew and of course witch grass, but do be aware that many of these do not press easily and some are quite poisonous to handle, so wear gloves.

A Sacred Space Symbol

Either purchase or make a wicker framework in a shape which you feel reflects your Craft – a pentacle, pentagon or crescent, for example. Then take a selection of dried plants and weave them into the frame. Lavender, rosemary and bay all make a good base. Then perhaps add jasmine for psychic energy, rowan for power, lily of the valley for strength, oak leaves for the God and lady's mantle for the Goddess. Of course these are just examples – there are numerous herbs, flowers and woods which are all significant in different ways.

If you wish you can also add other things to your symbol, perhaps a feather for Air, a crystal for Fire, a shell for Water and a stone with a hole in it for Earth. Alternatively, you can use this idea with fresh plants and change them to celebrate the seasonal festivals.

Give a House-Warming Picture to a Friend

Pressed flowers can be arranged on stiff card and held in place with a little clear glue and then framed behind glass. To bring someone good fortune in their new home you can use the same selection of plants as used in your sachet (*see above*), a selection from the 'Language of Flowers' list (*see above*), or a combination of the two. Try jasmine for love, rosemary for protection, red geranium for friendship, mint for warmth of feeling or marjoram for happiness, or simply choose a selection of flowers which you feel will please the recipient and imbue them Magically as a charm for the home.

Make a Memorial Bookmark

To commemorate an event, pressed flowers can be laid on a small sheet of card and covered with self-adhesive plastic to make a bookmark. In this way you have a tangible reminder of perhaps your wedding day, the birth of a child, the passing of a loved one, your child's coming of age, or even (for young ones), a birthday or special treat. In fact pressed flower arranging is an excellent way of introducing younger members of the family to the uses of flowers and herbs, as it involves glue and scissors and all those things a small child likes to mess with during the holidays.

There is no limit to the things you can make with dried or pressed plants and it is something of a shame that this very traditional way of carrying on the fruits of one season to the next has lost much of its popularity, mostly, I feel, because of the gaudy dyed flowers you see so often in shops of Ye Olde Gifte variety.

Terms and Definitions

'Do not be ignorant of me...'

Some of the words in this glossary have only been touched upon briefly in the text but are words which are in common use in the Craft and may well crop up in other books you have read or will read. Other words are also in common usage but have a particular meaning within the Craft, and that is the meaning I have given here.

Athame

The Witches' knife or blade. Traditionally a black-handled knife with a double-edged blade nine inches long, the Athame is used when invoking and banishing the elements and other energies. The only thing an Athame should cut is air, or the wedding cake at a Handfasting.

Besom

The traditional Witches' broomstick. On one hand this is a symbol of fertility which is literally jumped during a Handfasting to signify the leap from one 'life' to the next. The Besom is also used symbolically to sweep the Circle.

Boline

The white-handled knife. This is the working knife of the Witch and is used whenever any cutting, say, of herbs, or carving of symbols is required.

Book of Shadows

A personal record or journal of Magical workings and the thoughts, feelings and results that come from them. Gardnerian Witches refer to The Book of Shadows which was written by Gerald Gardner together with some of his senior Coven members.

Chalice

A symbol of the Goddess. The Chalice can be made from wood, stone, glass or metal and can be plain or ornate. What is important is that it contains the wine used in the Rite of Wine and Cakes, or in the Great Rite.

Circle

This defines the Sacred Space of the Witch. It is created whenever and wherever it is needed. Casting the Circle is just one part of creating the Sacred Space. A Coven would traditionally cast a Circle nine feet across; however, when working on your own it should be as small or large as your needs.

Coven

A group of three or more Witches (two would be a partnership). Coven size varies considerably, although some consider that a 'proper' Coven should be made up of six men, six women and the High Priestess. The Coven is the family group of the Witches.

Craft

One of the terms for Witchcraft, which has been rightly described as both an Art and a Craft.

Dark Mirror

A curved disc of glass painted black on the reverse to produce a reflecting surface. Alternatively, a bowl of water to which some black ink has been added. The Dark Mirror is used for divination or scrying.

Deity

A Goddess or a God. The term 'Deities' is often used generically for all Goddesses and Gods, wherever they have come from.

Deosil

Clockwise or Sunwise. When setting up and working in your Sacred Space you should always move Deosil, unless you are undoing something.

Divination

The techniques and ability to discover that which might otherwise remain hidden to us. The Tarot, crystal ball, astrology and tealeaves are all forms of divination. Witches tend to use the term 'scrying', although strictly speaking this refers to the Dark Mirror, Cauldron, Fire or Witches' Runes.

Divine

A broader term than 'Deity', the Divine encompasses both the Goddess and the God and includes those aspects which do not have a gender or a name.

Elements

The term 'elements' is often used to refer to Earth, Air, Fire and Water. However it is important that the fifth element, that of Spirit, which we ourselves bring to the Circle, is not forgotten. The elements are the keystones of the Craft and also refer to aspects of ourselves as well as energies around us.

Esbat

The Witches' term for Full Moon meetings or workings.

Goddess and God

The female and male aspects of the Divine. 'The Gods' is often used to denote both.

Great Rite

The symbolic union of the Goddess and the God. Generally, it is performed with the Chalice and Athame, the exceptions to this are between working partners and in some forms of initiation.

Handfasting

One of many Rites of Passage, Handfasting is the name for the Witches' wedding. It differs from most 'orthodox' kinds of wedding in that both parties enter as equals and make their own individual vows to each other. Handfastings can be of different prearranged durations.

High Priestess/High Priest

The leader of a Coven is usually the High Priestess. She may lead jointly with her High Priest, but holds ultimate authority and responsibility. Some groups are run by the High Priest alone, usually where there is no female of sufficient experience to take this role.

Initiation

'Initiation' literally means 'to begin'. However, in the Craft Initiation is seen as the permanent declaration an individual makes to their Gods. Many of the paths within the Craft refer to three degrees of initiation, each denoting a different level of attainment and ability.

Lore

Knowledge handed down from generation to generation. Originally an oral tradition, a lot of the old lore is now finding its way into books. Much ancient lore which was thought, in our scientific age, to be superstition, is now being proven and accepted.

Magic

The ability to create change by force of will. It is worth remembering that many things we take for granted, like electricity, would have been considered Magic by our ancestors.

Occult

Literally 'hidden'; in medicine 'occult blood' refers to blood that has been found through testing because it cannot be seen with the naked eye. Today the word is often used as a semi-derogatory term for anything which is not understood and is therefore feared.

Orthodox

A term I have used to identify those beliefs which people tend to think of as older than the supposedly New Age beliefs, when in fact the reverse can be said to be true. For example, people tend to think that Christianity is an older belief system than the modern Pagan beliefs, when in fact the origins of Paganism (including Witchcraft) vastly predate Christianity.

Pagan

A generic term for members of a number of pre-Christian religions – Druids, Witches and Heathens to name a few. Pagan probably comes from either the word paganus, referring to those who didn't live in the towns – a version of 'country-bumpkin' if you like – or from the word pagus, an administrative unit used by the occupying government. Either way it was originally used as an insult. Now it is a label worn by many with pride.

Pathworking

A form of guided meditation in which you take a journey which leads to an opportunity to discover more than you already know. Sometimes also referred to as 'interactive guided meditation'.

Pentacle

A five-pointed star with the points touching but not overlapping a circle. It symbolizes the five elements together with the Circle of power. The Pentacle is worn by many Witches, but is also currently very fashionable, so you cannot be sure whether the wearer is of the Craft or not.

Pentagram

A five-pointed star not enclosed in a circle (see Pentacle above).

Priest and/or Priestess

In the Craft we are each our own Priest or Priestess and need no one to intercede with or interpret our Gods for us.

Quarters

The four cardinal points of the compass – north, south, east and west – which are linked to the directions of the elements.

Reincarnation

To believe in reincarnation is to believe that we return to this world many times, as many different individuals.

Rite

A small piece of ritual which although complete in itself is not generally performed on its own, such as the Rite of Wine and Cakes. A series of rites put together are a ritual.

Rites of Passage

Rites that mark the change from one stage of life to another, such as birth, marriage and death. Their names in the Craft – Wiccaning, Handfasting and Withdrawal – are different from those in current use, which reflects the different emphasis that Witches place on these events. There are other Rites of Passage but they are less common even in the Craft today.

Ritual

A series of rites put together to achieve a specific result.

Sabbat

A seasonal festival. There are eight Sabbats in the Witches' calendar which together are often referred to as 'the Wheel of the Year'. Sabbats are traditionally times of great celebration and festivity. Many of the old Sabbats are still celebrated under more modern names – Yule is known as Christmas and Samhain as Halloween, for example.

Sacred Space

For many religions their place of worship, or religious centre, is a building. Witches create their Sacred Space wherever and whenever they need it, and their Magical workings, and some of their celebrations, take place within its boundaries.

Scrying

The Witches' term for divination, especially when carried out using a Dark Mirror or the Witches' Runes.

Spells and Spellcraft

A spell is a set of actions and/or words designed to bring about a specific Magical intent. Spellcraft is the ability, knowledge and wisdom to know when, as well as how, to perform such actions.

Strong Hand

For a person who is right-handed this will be their right hand, for someone who is left-handed it is their left. The strong hand is sometimes called 'the giving hand'.

Summerlands

The Witches' name for the place our spirit goes to between incarnations, where we rest and meet those who have gone before us and choose the lessons we will learn in our next life.

Thurible

Also known as a censer, this is a fireproof container designed to hold burning charcoal and loose incense.

Visualization

Seeing with the mind's eye so strongly that it appears no different from 'reality'. Visualization is not just about seeing, though – when you are skilled at it, all your senses will be involved. For example, when visualizing the element of Air you will feel the wind touch your hair and skin, hear its passage through the trees and smell the scents of spring. Visualization is one of the key factors in working the Craft and performing Magic.

Wand

A piece of wood the length of its owner's forearm. In some traditions the Wand is only used where the Athame is not, in others the Wand and Athame can be interchanged.

Wicca and Wiccan

Wicca has been largely adopted as a more 'user-friendly' term for Witchcraft. Personally I do not describe myself as a Wiccan as it simply leads to the question 'What does that mean?' and then you will sooner or later end up leading to the word 'Witch'. There are some who consider that those who call themselves Wiccans are less traditional than Witches.

Widdershins

Anticlockwise, the opposite to Deosil.

Witches' Runes

A series of eight stones with symbols representing fertility, union, conflict, distance, life, stasis, the Sun and the Moon, which are used for divination.

Further Information

'Merry Meet, Merry Part and Merry Meet Again!'

 Recommended Reading

There are a great many excellent books available today on the Craft, on cookery and on the uses of plants and herbs. I have not tried to list them all here but have selected those which I have found useful. Some are more general, while others specialize in a particular area which is too complex to be covered in an all-round text. If a book is not listed here it does not mean it is not a valuable work, nor is it intended as a slight to the author. Equally, not every book here will suit every reader, as each person has their own requirements in terms of content and preferences when it comes to style. If you find yourself reading something you find tedious or 'heavy going', do not feel that you have a problem – it may simply be that you and that work are not compatible.

You may find some of these books are out of print. However, it should be possible with perseverance to locate them through the library system. In any case, I would always recommend trying to get hold of a book through a library, at least in the first instance, as in this way you can see whether you like it before deciding to own a copy.

Books Especially Relevant to This Book

★ Scott Cunningham, *Cunningham's Encyclopaedia of Magical Herbs*, Llewellyn, 1985.
Magical uses and tales surrounding most common herbs.

★ — *Cunningham's Encyclopaedia of Crystal, Gem and Metal Magic*, Llewellyn, 1988.
Magical properties of most gemstones available today.

★ — *The Complete Book of Oils, Incenses and Brews*, Llewellyn, 1989.
Magical preparation and use of oils, incenses and other mixtures.

★ Allison England, *Aromatherapy for Mother and Baby*, Vermilion, 1993.
Gives safe and sensible advice for the use of aromatherapy oils during pregnancy
and childbirth and for babies.

★ Marian Green, A *Calendar of Festivals*, Element Books, 1991. Descriptions of festivals,
not just Pagan or Wiccan, around the year with practical things to do, make and cook.

★ Mrs M. Grieve, A *Modern Herbal*, Jonathan Cape, 1931; reissued Tiger, 1992.
A detailed reference for the serious herbalist; identification, preparation and use
of herbs, ancient and modern. Also available on the Internet at
http://www.botanical.com/botanical/mgmh/mgmh.html.

★ Barbara Griggs, *The Green Witch*, Vermilion, 1993.
More of a modern healer's handbook than a Magical reference book.

★ Claire Loewenfeld and Philippa Back, *Herbs for Health and Cookery*, Pan, 1965.
Ways of using household herbs.

★ *Folklore Myths and Legends of Britain*, Readers Digest Association Ltd, 1973.
Myths, folklore, festivals and customs around Britain by region.

★ Joanna Sheen, *Herbal Gifts*, Ward Lock, 1991.
A multitude of things to do with dried flowers and herbs.

★ Christina Westwood, *Aromatherapy*, Amberwood Publishing Ltd, 1991.
A quick and easy reference for aromatherapy oils.

★ Bill Whitcomb, *The Magician's Companion*, Llewellyn, 1993. Possibly the ultimate
reference work for correspondences and symbols.

General Books on the Craft

★ J. W. Baker, *The Alex Sanders Lectures*, Magickal Childe, 1984.
A perspective on Alexandrian Witchcraft.

★ Rae Beth, *Hedgewitch*, Phoenix, 1990. Solitary Witchcraft,
written as a series of letters to newcomers.

★ Janice Broch and Veronica MacLer, *Seasonal Dance*, Weiser, 1993.
New ideas for the Sabbats.

★ Janet and Stewart Farrar, A *Witches' Bible* (formerly *The Witches' Way* and
Eight Sabbats for Witches), Phoenix, 1996. Alexandrian Craft as it is practised.

★ Gerald Gardner, *The Meaning of Witchcraft*, Rider & Co., 1959;
reissued by Magickal Childe, 1991. Gardnerian Witchcraft.

★ Pattalee Glass-Koentop, *Year of Moons, Season of Trees*, Llewellyn, 1991.
Information on the tree calendar and ideas to incorporate at the Full Moons.

★ Paddy Slade, *Natural Magic*, Hamlyn, n.d. A perspective on Traditional Witchcraft.

★ Doreen Valiente, ABC *of Witchcraft*, Hale, 1973.
Gardnerian Craft written in 'dictionary' format.

★ Kate West, *The Real Witches' Handbook*, HarperCollins, 2000.
Real Witchcraft for real people with real lives, this book shows how to practise
the Craft in a way sensitive to those around you.

★ Kate West and David Williams, *Born in Albion: The Re-Birth of the Craft*,
Pagan Media Ltd, 1996. An introduction to the Craft from the Coven perspective.
Note this book will soon be out of print.

Specialist Books on Aspects of the Craft

★ Anne Llewellyn Barstow, *Witchcraze*, HarperCollins, 1995.
Detailed history of the persecution of Witches.

★ Jean Shinola Bolen, *Goddesses in Everywoman*, HarperCollins, 1985. A guide to finding the Goddess within and a wealth of tales about the aspects of the Goddess.

★ Janet and Stewart Farrar, *The Witches' Goddess*, Hale, 1987.
Examination of some of the more common Goddesses.

★ — *The Witches' God*, Hale, 1989. Examination of some of the more common Gods.

★ Paul Katzeff, *Moon Madness*, Citadel, 1981. A study of the effects of the Moon and many of the legends and mythology associated with it.

★ Patricia Monaghan, *The Book of Goddesses and Heroines*, Llewellyn, 1981.
A definitive guide to major and minor Goddesses from around the world.

★ Jeffrey B. Russell, *A History of Witchcraft*,
Thames and Hudson, 1983. A factual history of the Craft.

★ Egerton Sykes, *Who's Who: Non-Classical Mythology*, Oxford University Press, 1993.
A dictionary of Gods and Goddesses.

★ Tybol, *Tybol Astrological Almanac*, annual publication. Diary containing detailed astrological information, Goddess and God festivals, Magical terms and much more.

★ Kate West, *Pagan Paths*, Pagan Media Ltd, 1997.
Six Pathworking audio-cassettes covering the elements, the Goddess and the God.

★ — *Pagan Rites of Passage*, Mandrake Press, 1997.
A series of booklets giving information and rituals for Rites of Passage.

Points of Contact

The following organizations facilitate contact or provide information on Witchcraft and Paganism. Please always enclose a stamped self-addressed envelope and remember that some of these organizations may not allow membership to people under the age of 18. (For further information on getting in touch safely with other Witches or groups, please see the advice in *The Real Witches' Handbook*.)

The Children of Artemis

The UK's foremost witchcraft organisation. Initiated Witches who seek to find reputable training Covens for genuine seekers. Their magazine, *Witchcraft and Wicca*, has been rated one of the best on the Craft today.

BM Box Artemis, London WC1N 3XX.

http://www.witchcraft.org <contact@witchcraft.org>

ASLaN

Information on the care and preservation of Sacred Sites all over Britain.

http://www.symbolstone.org/archaeology/aslan. <andy.norfolk@connectfree.co.uk

The Hearth of Hecate

The author's group of Covens which can be contacted by writing to the author care of the publishers.

The Witches' Voice

One of the best American sources of information about the Craft.

PO Box 4924, Clearwater, FL 33758-4924, USA.

http://www.witchvox.com

The Pagan Federation

One of the foremost Pagan organizations in Europe, whose magazine, *Pagan Dawn*, provides information on events and contact details for some groups. Members include Witches, Druids, Shamans, those of the Northern Traditions and other Pagan paths.

BM Box 7097, London WC1N 3XX. http://www.paganfed.org

Inform

Totally independent and not aligned to any religious organization or group, Inform's primary aim is to help people by providing them with accurate, objective and up-to-date information on new religious movements, alternative religions, unfamiliar belief systems and 'cults'.

Houghton Street, London WC2A 2AE; Tel. 00 44 (0)20 7955 7654

Index